Spells from the
Wise Woman's Cottage

An Introduction to the West Country
Cunning Tradition

SPELLS
from the
Wise Woman's Cottage

Being a monograph on the history of the 'Wise Woman's Cottage' in the Museum of Witchcraft & Magic, in the maritime village of Boscastle in the county of Cornwall and a true and accurate account of the charms and words spoken therein. Recorded by the unflinching hand of your humble servant, Steve Patterson, over candlemas in the year of our Lord MMXVI

TROY BOOKS

© Steve Patterson 2016

First printed in paperback 2017

ISBN 978-1-909602-20-5

Published by Troy Books
www.troybooks.co.uk

Troy Books Publishing
BM Box 8003
London WC1N 3XX

Cover design: Gemma Gary

Contents

Photo Plates
Between Pages 80 - 81

Familliar spirit animals of 'The Wise Woman's Cottage'

Painted egg shell and 'conker' charms hung from the beams of the cottage.

Pin-cushion heart charm.

A rope of magical knots on the wise woman's table.

A raggy wreath charm from a Devon coven, and the alcove set with a carved slate from the Cecil Williamson collection.

'Old Joan' with the tools of her tade.

Photography by Jane Cox

INTRODUCTION

This volume is intended to serve two purposes. Firstly it is intended to work as an accompaniment to the 'Wise Woman's Cottage' tableau in the Museum of Witchcraft and Magic in Boscastle, Cornwall. Secondly, I hope it will stand as a book in its own right and serve as a general introduction to folk-magic practices, cunning traditions and witchcraft in the West Country. The book falls into three sections:

Old Joan's Book of Spells

The first is a transcription of the spells and charms you hear being spoken in the 'Wise Woman's Cottage' display. They are all genuine charms used by the old wayside witches and cunning folk.

Most of them were collected in the West Country in the 18th, 19th and early-20th centuries, and all of them would have been familiar to the cunning folk and the sea-witches of Boscastle 100 years ago. This is one of the most comprehensive collections of West Country cunning charms to date and I am sure it will be of interest to many but, for those who wish to use this as a working book of spells, be aware that these are all actual cunning charms!

A Guide to the 'Wise Woman's Cottage'

The second section serves as a guide book to the 'Wise Woman's Cottage' tableau in the Museum of Witchcraft and Magic. You will find that it contains much previously-unpublished material from the museum archives, from the former proprietors of the museum and from the author's own researches. However, it will also serve as a sourcebook of folk-magic and cunning practices in the West Country.

Witchcraft, the 'Wise Woman's Cottage' 🙖 *and the West Country Cunning Tradition*

The third section will provide you with a background to the Museum of Witchcraft and Magic, including the strange tale of the construction of the 'Wise Woman's Cottage' itself, and most importantly, an introduction to some ideas about Wicca, witchcraft and cunning traditions in the West Country.

Whether you read this as a book of magical practices, or an enquiry into our social history or just a good old spooky yarn, is entirely up to you. The world of magic is a strange and fascinating place, and it is rarely what one thinks it to be. As Tertullian once said:

"Certum est quia impossibile est" – *"It is certain because it is impossible!"*

Steve Patterson, Cornwall,
Plough Monday 2016

OLD JOAN'S BOOK OF SPELLS

*Some 19th Century
West Country Cunning Charms*

In the 'Wise Woman's Cottage' you will hear an imagined monologue from a 19th-century white witch or 'peller' to a client or a curious antiquarian. But make no mistake – these are all genuine charms, told by genuine cunning folk and collected in the West Country by genuine antiquarians in the late-19th and early-20th centuries.

Imagine the scene – a small granite cottage, just outside the village, on the edge of the moors somewhere in North Cornwall. He, the visitor, comes from a brave new urban world of science and reason while our cunning woman is from the tail end of a fading lineage in a vanishing rural world. And, sure enough, after two world wars and the onset of modernity, by the middle of the 20th century, the wayside witch and the communities that she served were all but gone. Much of what we know of the ways of the old cunning folk may well have come from encounters such as this. You, like the antiquarians that came before you, may be surprised by the content of some of the charms. They may not be the words you expect to hear, but as far as we know these are some of the charms that were actually used by the wayside witches.

I am sure you will agree that there is something both eerie and quite moving in hearing these voices from another age speaking to us from down the centuries. Just remember, as the old Devonshire wise woman once said to Cecil Williamson, the original founder of the Museum of Witchcraft and Magic:

"Look up, look up – there are other places and other things".

Magical Water Charms ❧

❧ **Charm for Washing Hands in the Moon's Rays:** Focus the moon's rays into an empty wash basin. Wash and dry your hands, then fill the basin with water and allow it to come to stillness. Next immerse your face in the reflection of the moon, kissing the bottom of the basin and taking in some of the water through your mouth. Then lift up your head and look directly at the full moon and, as you wash your hands again in the water in the dish, say:

"I wash my hands in this thy dish, Oh, man in the moon, do grant my wish, for I have kissed thee in thy dish".

Then take the basin of water and cast it to the moon.

❄ **Magic Charm Water:** Gather nine spar stones (quartz) from a running stream, taking care not to disturb the free flow of the stream. Then dip a quart of water from the stream. This must be taken in the direction in which the stream runs; on no account must the vessel be dipped against the flow of the stream.

Make the stones red hot and drop them in to a quart of water. Bottle the prepared water and use for the purposes desired.

Love Spells ❧

❄ **Divination Charm to Find a Lover:**

"All hail, all hail to thee,
All hail to thee, new moon!
I pray to thee, new moon,

Before thou growest old,
To reveal unto me who my true love shall be."

❧ Hempseed Divination Charm: At midnight I cast the hempen seed and chant this charm that my true love I shall see:

"Hempseed I sow, hempseed I hoe
In hopes that my true love
Will come after me and mow".

❧ Charm for Lovers:

"Good night fair yarrow,
thrice goodnight to thee;
I hope before tomorrow's dawn,
my true love I shall see."

❧ A Knitting Spell:

"This knot I knit,
To know the thing I know not yet,
That I may see the man who shall my husband be;
How he goes and what he wears,
And what he does, all days, and all years."

❧ A Charm to Stir your Lover's Heart by the Burning of 'Dragon's Blood':

Buy three pennyworth of 'dragon's blood' from the apothecary. Take no food or drink all day, and then at midnight take the 'dragon's blood' wrapped in white paper and burn it, keeping the name of your lover in your mind. Then speak this charm:

"Dragon's blood, dragon's blood,
'Tis not your blood I wish to burn,
But my true love's heart I wish to turn.
May he never sleep, rest, nor happy be
Until he comes, and send to me."

❧ A Love Spell:

Upon All Hallows' Eve, I write these words upon an apple:

"Coamer, Synady, Heupide."

And then I say:

"I conjure thee apple, by these three names written on thee, that whosoever shall eat thee shall burn in my love."

❧ **Charm for Beauty of Skin & Firm Flesh & Breasts:** At midnight, when the September moon is full, strip naked and go to an apple tree and climb up in to it. Take the topmost apple you can reach, then, face the moon placing your feet wide apart, one on a limb to the left of the main trunk and one to the right of same. In this position raise your face to the moon, and with outstretched arms holding the apple, intone your wish and give praise to the moon. Then eat the apple, every bit of it. Climb down and run round the tree nine times from left to right. Go home and go to bed naked without washing your hands or feet.

Healing Spells ⚬

⚬ A Devonshire Charm for Warts: Warts and swellings are removed by various charms, such as using skeins of thread, knotted with the number of warts to be removed, which is struck across the warts as many times, and then buried; or striking with a wych elm wand, or a piece of stolen bacon, which are also buried. As the buried article decays so do the warts gradually decrease; but the favourite remedy for warts, and indeed all swellings, is to have 'words' said over them.

⚬ Another Devonshire Charm for Warts: Sing this once to the left ear then to the right, and then to the poll (head). Then let one who is a maiden hang this upon the sufferer's neck for three days, then it will soon be well with him.

"Here came entering a spider wight,
He had his hands upon his hams;
He quoth that thou his hackney wert.

Lay thee against his neck.
They began to sail of the land;
As soon as they of the land came,
Then they began to cool.
Then came a wild beast's sister;
Then she ended.
And oaths she swore that never could
This harm the sick, nor him who could get at
This charm, nor him who had skill to sing this charm.
Amen!"

✣ Fever Charm:

"In the name of St Exuperus and St Honorius,
fall-fever, spring-fever, Quartain, quintain, ago,
super ago, consummatum est."

✣ Charm for Wildfire:

"Christ He walketh over the land, carried the
wildfire in His hand, He rebuked the fire and
made it stand: stand wildfire stand.
(Repeat three times)
In the name of the Father, the Son and the
Holy Ghost."

❦ Charm for a Scald:

"Three ladies came from the East,
One with fire and two with frost;
Out with thee fire, and in with thee frost.
In the name of the Father, the Son and the
Holy Ghost."

❦ Charm for a Bruise:

"Holy chi-chi! Holy chi-chi!
This bruise will get well by-and-by.
Up sun high and down moon low,
This bruise will be quite well soon-oh!
In the name of the Father, the Son and the
Holy Ghost."

❦ Charm for Tetters:

"Tetter, tetter, thou has nine sisters.
God bless thee flesh and preserve thee bone.
Perish thee tetter and be thou gone.
In the name of the Father, the Son and the
Holy Ghost."

❦ Charm for a Strain:

"Christ rode over the bridge,
Christ rode under the bridge;
Vein to vein, strain to strain,
I hope God will take it back again."

❦ Blessing for a Sting of a Long-Cripple (Snake):

"Yender under a halsin (hazel) mote there lays
a great braget worm nine double, nine double
to eight double, seven double to six double, five
double to four double, three double to two double,
one double and to no double.
In the name of the Father, the Son and the
Holy Ghost."
(Repeat three times)

❦ For Stenting (Staunching) Blood:

"As Christ was born in Bethlehem and was baptised
in the river of the fair water Jordan, this water was
wild and rude, with a rod still it stood – and so pray
Christ grant the blood may stop. In the name of the
Father, the Son and the Holy Ghost."

❧ **Charm for Kennel of the Eye:** As I rub the kenning-stone upon your eye, this charm I shall intone:

"Simon and Gaus went to our Lord Jesus Christ and asked him what to do against pins, pearls and webs. Our Lord and Saviour, Jesus Christ, answered and said:
Simon and Gaus, from your eyes let red fall; from your eyes let black fall. Eyes be eyes! Eyes be eyes! Eyes be eyes!
In the name of the Father, the Son and the Holy Ghost."

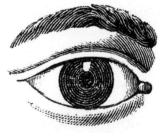

❧ **General Purpose Charm:**

"Holy kai, Holy kei,
(Tommy's nose) will be better by and by.
Up sun, down moon,
(Tommy's nose) will be better soon."

Protection Spells 🐛

🐛 To be Said While Nailing into a Post:

"Feyther, Son and Holy Ghost,
Naal the divil to this post!
Throis I stroiks with holy crook;
Won for God, won for Wod and won for lok."

🐛 To be Said While Nailing a Horseshoe to a Door: As I nail a horseshoe to the door, this I chant:

"So as the fire do melt the wax
And wind blows the smoke away,
So in the presence of the Lord
The wicked shall decay, the wicked shall decay.
Amen."

❦ Charm for Protection: I write these words upon this charm:

"SATOR, AREPO, TENET, OPERA, ROTAS – Jehovah, Jah, Eloim, Shadday, Adonay, Have mercy on a poor woman".

❦ Charm for Recovering Stolen Goods (found carved on a roofing slate):

*"May he who stole my round stones
Return, repent and make dry bones."*

❦ A Charm to Turn Back the 'Evil Eye': If you have been ill-wished, take an apple, a potato or a bullock's heart, stick it with pins, hang it up the chimney and let it dry and shrivel. As it turns, so will the 'Evil Eye' return to its sender.

�֍ A Charm to Restore Lost Money:

"Flibberty, gibberty, flasky flum;
Calafac tarada, lara, wagra wum.
Hooky, maroosky, whatever the sum,
Heigho! Presto! Money come.
In the name of the Father, the Son and the Holy
Ghost."

Witchcraft ֍

�֍ Another Charm for Washing Hands in the Moon's Rays:

"I wash my hands in this thy dish,
Oh man in the moon, do grant my wish,
And come and take away this."

�֍ **Club Moss Charm:** This stuff is good! It can be used for diseases of the eyes and many other purposes but it must be cut on the third day of the new moon, when the crescent is thin and seen for the first time. Show the moon the knife with which the moss is to be cut. Your hands must have been washed in cold water at sundown and the moss must be cut while you are kneeling. It must be carefully wrapped in a clean, white cloth with a black spot in the centre of same. Then the moss is to be washed in water taken from the nearest spring or stream to the point of gathering, being careful to observe the rules of the taking of water. This fluid can then be used as a wash or fermentation, or the moss may be mixed with fresh butter and made into an ointment for many uses, chief of which is its use for the delights of love-making.

❦ How to Become a Witch: To become a witch you must first have the 'virtue', and that gives you the power of the peller. Sometimes the 'virtue' is passed down in the family or a line of witches: man to woman or woman to man. Sometimes it appears if you are the seventh child of a seventh child, and sometimes you can bring it on by touching one of the old logan stones nine times at midnight.

❧ Witches' Chant: And when I gather with my sisters in the fogou dark, this merry charm we chant!

"I have knit and spun for thee
For three years and a day;
Tomorrow I will ride with thee,
Over the land and over the sea.
Far away! Far away!
For we shall ever know
That thy name is 'Tarraway'.
By night and day, we will dance and play,
With our noble captain – Tarraway, Tarraway."

"Here's to the Devil,
With his wooden spade and shovel,
Digging tin by the bushel
With his tail cocked up!"

A Word to the Would-be Wayside Witch ❧

There you have it: a representation of a traditional old-time wayside witch and her works. Cecil Williamson often spoke of what he called 'the silent world of witchcraft'. One could interpret this on many levels. First and foremost he used it as a way of describing the twilight world of the wayside witches, working quietly in their communities, away from the public eye. Second, it could be said to refer to the unseen and indeed unknowable aspect of the magical work of the witch, which must forever remain shrouded in the mists of the spirit world, for this is the ineffable nature of true magic.

So where do these spoken spells and charms fit in to all this, I hear you ask? Indeed, that is for you if you so wish, to find out for yourself. As the old man himself was once heard to say when an over-eager visitor to the museum asked why he avoided making any simple explanations of magic: *"There would be no point in making it too easy!"*

If you do feel the urge to try for yourself one of the charms described in this book, just be aware of a few things. First, these spells were part of a tradition that required wisdom and many years of experience. You must take responsibility for what you stir up; the charms always work, though quite often not in the way you think! It is rarely ghosties or ghoulies or long-legged beasties in the night that cause you problems; it is yourself you have to look out for! The keystone of all magic, and indeed one could say the whole point of life, is to 'Know Thyself' – for that is what you conjure into the world.

Remember the words of the old wayside witch:

"Be careful what you ask for, you might just get it!"

Notes & Commentary on the Charms ᚫ

Here are a few notes on the charms and spells in this volume. I have attempted to list some of the sources and other versions that appear and I think it is made clear that these charms, far from being the creation of a romantic antiquarian or a deluded individual, were part of an extensive witch-belief that survived into the modern period. The origins of some appear to go back at least a thousand years.

Charm for Washing Hands in the Moon's Rays, p.17

(Source J) An almost-identical charm is mentioned by Courtney (Source F) and Bottrell (Source G) as a charm to remove warts. Interestingly, Bottrell suggests that this may have a Phoenician origin. A similar charm can also be found in the work of the 18th-century polymath Sir Kenelm Digby (who was also a pirate, an alchemist, and invented the wine bottle) in his treatise on sympathetic magic.

Magic Charm Water, p.18

This tradition is recorded by Hunt (p416), Courtney (p161) and Paynter (p100) as being a cure for whooping cough, but its elements belie a deeper magical significance. Quartz has been used as a magical object since the Neolithic period in Cornwall. 'Holy water' was widely used for its curative and spiritual virtues in Roman Catholic Britain, but since the Reformation its use and method of production seems to have moved into the realm of the cunning artes!

Divination Charm to Find a Lover, p.18
(Source B) New moon charms are as ubiquitous as the grass. Its virtues have long been held to have influence over the realms of love, dreams and magic. Similar versions to this Devonshire charm appear in the 17th-century works of John Aubrey (Source C) and the 18th-century works of astrologer and fortune-teller, Ebenezer Sibly.

Hempseed Divination Charm, p.19
(Source D) This charm was said at midnight in the graveyard while the hempseed was thrown over one's left shoulder. Hemp has many folkloric associations, most of which seem to be derived from its consciousness-altering properties. This charm has also been recorded in Oxfordshire and the Welsh Marches. In this Cornish version it is specifically connected with Midsummer, though in other versions it is recommended to be spoken on St Mark's Eve, All Hallows' Eve or Christmas Eve.

Charm for Lovers, p.19
(Source F) In this Cornish version of this herbal charm the operator plucks the yarrow at the new moon and places it under her pillow to inspire dreams of a future lover. Yarrow has many folkloric associations with divination. Similar charms frequently appear in the south of England.

A Knitting Spell, p.20
(Sources C and F) Cecil Williamson noted that the repetitive act of knitting was an ideal basis for spell-casting. This particular charm also turns up in the 18th-century popular works of Ebenezer Sibly.

A Charm to Stir your Lover's Heart by the Burning of 'Dragon's Blood', p.20
(Source H) Other variants of this charm appear around Britain. This version from East Cornwall employs the use of 'dragon's blood', made from the resin of the dragon tree, which is native to the Canary Islands. This was possibly imported to Cornwall in the 18th

century by the Enys family. Mr Paynter, the collector of the charm, had a small business in selling this as a charm to would-be lovers!

A Love Spell, p.20
(Source H) This charm seems unique to East Cornwall. The Latin-sounding charm is reminiscent of those used in the 18th-century 'grimoire' The Black Pullet.

The apple in Northern European folklore has often been associated with love spells and the Celtic Otherworld, and charms employing the apple for various forms of divination have been used at Halloween throughout Britain.

Charm for Beauty of Skin & Firm Flesh & Breasts, p.21
(Source J) Here is another idiosyncratic rite with apparently no precedent. It was collected from Cecil Williamson, with his characteristic attention to the logistical details of the magical operation, suggesting that this is something that he may actually have done himself. Paynter suggests that Cornish folklore dictates

that the apple is particularly susceptible to the influence of the moon, and if picked on a waning moon it will end up 'shrumped up'. Thus, theoretically, the picking of the apple on the full moon will at least keep the apple firm and fresh! The use of the moon, the apple and the naked nine-fold perambulations of the tree are all classic ingredients to a West Country cunning charm.

A Devonshire Charm for Warts, p.22
From the Transactions of the Devonshire Society (1897) – a fine repository of folkloric gems! The formula of the transference of the warts to an external object (contagious magic), and then employing some force to decay the said object (sympathetic magic) in order to destroy the original warts is found in a myriad of different charms throughout Britain.

Another Devonshire Charm for Warts, p.22
(Source H) This must be one of the strangest and eeriest spells in the Paynter collection. I have found no other version of this, though it is somewhat reminiscent

of the spells used by the Anglo-Saxons (such as the spell for banishing 'wens') in which the cause of the illness was first mythologised, then zoomorphised into the form of a creature, and then destroyed by the shaman/sorcerer.

Fever Charm, p.23
(Source B) This Devonshire charm uses a form and a Latin-esque language that pertains to the medieval 'grimoires, though it doesn't seem to be derived from any one in particular. The saints venerated by the common people were by no means only the ones sanctioned by the Roman Catholic Church; there were a great number of vernacular 'folk' saints, and these often turn up in folk-magic. St Exuperus may be the man who was Bishop of Toulouse at the beginning of the 5th century, and St Honorius must be none other than the infamous pope Honorius III, who is credited with being versed in the magical artes and of penning the infamous 14th-century 'grimoire' The Sworn Book of Honorius.

Charm for Wildfire, p.23
(Sources D and F) Wildfire was the old name for Erysipelas, also known as 'St Anthony's Fire', which is a bacterial skin infection. It seems that many charmers practised this charm. On the surface this spell seems to be Christian, but the episode to which it refers is legendary.

Charm for a Scald, p.24
(Source B, D, E, G, H, I and K) This charm appears in a great number of variant forms and purposes. For example Bottrell cites a version used to break a curse. It could be said to be a multi-purpose Pellars Blessing! It is often ended with the benediction - "In the name of the Father, the Son and the Holy Ghost", but the previous part of the charm seems to be referencing an entirely non-Christian mythological incident. Some have speculated it is about the stages of the sun as it passes through the sky; dawn, midday and dusk. Some have speculated it is of Anglo-Saxon origin and may refer to the three Norns or fates of the northern tribes.

Charm for a Bruise, p.24
(source B) R Morton Nance sites two similar versions of this Devonshire charm from Camborne and St Ives in West Cornwall in the 1920s. He speculates that "Holy chichi" is derived from the Cornish "Woly ky ky", meaning "Wound go, go".

Charm for Tetters, p.24
(source F, G and K) Tetters are the old name for skin problems such as rashes or blisters. The Charm proceeds by counting down less and less – "Tetter, Tetter thou has eight sisters" etc., until there are none. Nine is the Pellars magic number it appears in many charms. The embodiment of the Tetter in an anthropomorphic form is a hint to the charms antiquity.

Charm for a Strain, p.25
(Source D, F and I) This charm is purely Anglo-Saxon in origin, it refers to a mythological incident in which Odin fell from his horse and was healed. In many versions he is replaced by Christ ...but the song remains the same.

Blessing for a Sting of a Long-Cripple, p.25
(Source A, D and F) There are many
variant forms of this charm. It seems to
be drawing on a mythological incident
in which a hazel rod destroys a snake.
The 10t century *'Nine Herbs Charm'*
relates –

"When Woden took nine twigs of
glory, then struck the adder so that it
flew in to nine pieces."

The charm seems to have been used
down the ages. Another Saxon charm
from the same period employs the
same counting down from nine to zero
formula; a version was even collected
in the 1980s by folklorist Rose Mullins
from Bodmin Moor in mid-Cornwall.

For Stenting (Staunching) Blood, p.25
(Sources A, D, E, F, I and K) On the
surface this charm also appears to be
Christian, but it draws on an entirely
mythical episode in which Christ stops
the flow of the River Jordan. It also
seems to have been in common usage
among the charmers. Folklorist, Theo
Brown, cites the trial of the Devonshire

witch Joan Ingra in Exeter in 1599 where it is claimed that she used a variant of this charm; and the folklorist Sabine Baring-Gould records its use by the Devon charmer, Mariann Voaden, at the end of the 19th century.

Charm for Kennel of the Eye, p.26
(Source E) This charm also seems to be referring to an apocryphal incident. It is unclear who Gaus is, but Simon could be the apostle. One cannot help but consider that 'Simon and Gaus' might be a mishearing on the part of the collector and that it might be none other than 'Simon Magus', considered by the early Christians to be the archetypal mountebank although he was a spiritual leader and possible rival to Jesus to the early Gnostics. It is surprising how many non-Biblical legends were in circulation and embedded in the folk-magic tradition. One can only assume that little distinction was made by ordinary people between the Bible and the vernacular Christian myths.

General Purpose Charm, p.26
(Source E) Canon Doble also collected a version of this charm in Glastonbury in the 1920s, from a woman whose mother came from Feock in Cornwall. Unlike R Morton Nance's interpretation of Charm 14, Doble speculates that it is invoking the intercession of the Cornish saint Kia (also known as Ke or Kea). By invoking the saints, the sun and the moon one can keep all one's bases covered!

To be Said While Nailing into a Post, p.27
An 1857 charm known on Bodmin moor and cited by folklorist Rose Mullins, it appears to be invoking the Anglo-Saxon gods Odin and Loki, in addition to the Christian god; maybe this harks back to a period when a dual faith was practised. The prevalence of the many Norse pagan elements of the cunning charms could be due in part to the fact that the Cornish so disliked the Saxons that for a period they allied themselves with the Danish Vikings, who were far more vociferous in their pagan leanings than the Saxons.

To be Said While Nailing a Horseshoe to a Door, p.27

(Source B) This is clearly a reference to Psalm 68: "As wax melteth, so the wicked perish". The use of the Psalms, either as a whole or by inference, is common in the charming tradition; in fact there are entire 'grimoires' dedicated to the magical use of the Psalms.

Charm for Protection, p28

(Source G) The palindrome of the 'SATOR' square has appeared as a charm since Roman times. It was also in use in the form of a written paper charm by the West Country cunning folk up to the 19th century. One can only assume that it was also used as a spoken charm as well. However, this particular charm's origins and meaning are obscure. In this context it seems to be invoking the protective aspect of Saturn, especially in relation to malefic spirits.

Charm for Recovering Stolen Goods, p.28

This charm was collected by the author; it was found scratched on to a roofing slate on a barn in West Cornwall and it probably dates from the turn of the 20th century. I have not found any similar examples, but it seems to be following a fairly typical charming formula. What the 'round stones' were, and as to whether they were ever recovered, we shall never know!

A Charm to Turn Back the 'Evil Eye', p.28
(Sources F,G,H,J and K) In the world of folk-magic, all the ills of the world can be attributed to the evil witch casting the 'Evil Eye', so there is a correspondingly large collection of charms to counteract it. Variants of this charm are found throughout Britain and evidence of it has been discovered secreted in the walls and fireplaces of many old houses.

A Charm to Restore Lost Money, p.29
(Source B) The opening line may be referring to the cry of Shakespeare's King Lear as he raves on the stormy heath; otherwise it appears to be a strange and childlike nonsense charm. One cannot but help entertain the idea that in this

instance the informant may have been leading the collector a merry dance!

Another Charm for Washing Hands in the Moon's Rays, p.29

(Source F) Another classic example utilising the moon, water and the wish of the operator bound into a charm.

Club Moss Charm, p.29

(Sources F, J and K) Courtney and Hunt claimed that it was for the curing of diseases of the eye. Williamson however recommends it for 'the delights of lovemaking'! This suggests that either this was the version he came across or that charms are a neutral technology that can be directed by the will of the operator. It also appears underlined in Cecil Williamson's copy of The Encyclopaedia of Superstitions – E and M A Radford (1947). In this account they add: "The operative clause seems to be the phrase '… if properly gathered', and it took the authors two months of enquiry to discover an old Cornishman who could tell the proper way to gather the club moss".

How to Become a Witch, p.30
(Sources J, G, F and K) The ways of becoming a witch are many and varied. Cecil Williamson claimed that it was all about getting a 'familiar' spirit. The idea of becoming a witch by obtaining the 'virtue' seems to be purely a West Country tradition. Whatever the theory, some kind of ritual act is usually employed, unless of course you are born to it.

Witches' Chant, p.31
(Source G) All these chants come from William Bottrell's account of the witches' Sabbat in his tale 'Duffy and the Devil'. One assumes he was drawing upon the folkloric beliefs of his time. Whatever their pedigree, as charms they remain eerie and evocative, and as to who the mysterious 'Tarraway' is … well that is another story!

Elaine Gill points out that, interestingly, 'Tarow' is the Cornish language word for 'bull'. Could this relate to the horned God? The leader of the coven featured in the 'Duffy and the Devil' story, was said to have met with the Devil in the form of a large black bull in St Buryan churchyard.

Sources of the Charms 🕭

SOURCE A

From *The Life and Letters of R S Hawker of Morwenstow* – C E Byles (1905). "The following are copied from a manuscript of an old (Morwenstow, Cornwall) parishioner."

SOURCE B

Quoted by Sarah Hewett in *Nummets and Crummets* (1900). Collected in Devon in the late-19th century and reprinted by Troy Books as *Devon Witchcraft and Folk Ways* (2009).

SOURCE C

From *Miscellanies on Various Subjects* – John Aubrey (1696).

SOURCE D

From *History of Polperro* – Jonathan Couch (1871). Mr Couch went to Polperro with the intention of working on his great opus on the study of fish. In his travels he fortuitously came across the most comprehensive collection of cunning charms (13 in number) ever collected in one place. He states:

"I happened once on a manuscript account book of a white witch or charmer ... towards the end were several charms and superstitious remedies. Risking the impropriety I copied the following ..."

SOURCE E
From *Randigal Rhymes and a Glossary of Cornish Words* – Joseph Thomas (1895). "Collected from a 'fortune-telling dame' in the West Penwith district."

SOURCE F
From *Cornish Feasts and Folklore* – M A Courtney (1886-7)
SOURCE G
William Bottrell
• *Hearthside Stories of West Cornwall* (1870)
• *Traditions & Hearthside Stories of West Cornwall* (1873)
• *Stories & Folklore of West Cornwall* (1880)

SOURCE H
• From *The Cornish Witch-finder* – William Henry Paynter, edited by Jason Semmens,

published by The Federation of Old Cornwall Societies (2008).

• A collection of the folklorist W. H. Paynter's papers, from charms collected mainly in East Cornwall in the mid-part of the 20th century.

SOURCE I

Devonshire Characters and Strange Events – Sabine Baring-Gould (1908). Charms collected from the notebook of Mariann Voaden, a 'white witch' from Bratton Clovelly, Devon in the late-19th century.

SOURCE J

Cecil Williamson's Book of Witchcraft – Steve Patterson, Troy Books (2014)

From a notebook of spells collected by Cecil Williamson, the founder of the Museum of Witchcraft, in the West Country in the mid-part of the 20th century.

SOURCE K

Popular Romances of the West of England – Robert Hunt (Penzance 1871)

A GUIDE TO THE
WISE WOMAN'S COTTAGE

WELCOME to Old Joan's Cottage. The wise woman sits at her table surrounded by the things that she uses to work her magical artes. Behind her in the hearth crackles her gorse fire. To the witch the hearth fire is not just a means of cooking and keeping warm, and the chimney is far more than just a means of drawing away the smoke. The witch's hearth fire is a shrine, a spirit-house, a gateway to the Otherworld and the focal point of all her magic. Seeing her sitting at her table one is put in mind of Cecil Williamson's own description of an old-time witch:

"These ladies are solo workers, they do not have to seek clients, for those with problems come knocking on their door. Payment is not sought or asked for, it is given by the client, and there are no tools of the trade or regalia, no covenstead decorated with symbols or signs. Natural objects such as twigs, stones and flowers etc are sometimes used."

Her magic has been worked for generations, and it still goes on today. Even now there are those who have the skills of wort-cunning, herb lore, blood staunching and all the other magical artes. Some of them are still in the villages and on the wild moors – and some of them are where you least expect to find them! The wise woman has little care for material wealth; those grateful for her services give her what they can afford, and if she is ever found wanting she is usually provided for by her friends in the spirit world, who are never far away.

If you look behind her on the far wall you will see a small alcove with a single candle. It is here that she makes her prayers and gives thanks to the 'Old Ones'. The stone at its back comes from Cecil Williamson's collection. It displays a number of diagonal grooves making a kind of grid. This pattern is typical of the prehistoric carvings sometimes found in caves and on ancient stones. It has been speculated that it represents the images that flicker across the shamans' eyes as they sink in to their Otherworldly, dreamlike trances.

Divination and Scrying 🜛

As you look through the door you will see old Joan with her crystal ball and her cards spread out before her. Much of the bread-and-butter work of the wise woman was the practice of divination or scrying. This was not just the art of looking into the future, but to be able to perceive the past, and most importantly to be able to see clearly in to the 'here and now'. Thus lost souls, lovers, thieves, treasure and mysteries could be found or solved.

"Unlike most people she is endowed with a third eye, which when one has learned to open and use – the same world becomes an entirely different place."

The wise woman doesn't need expensive tools; an old green glass fishing float steeped in the powers of the sea works just as well as any fancy crystal ball. She is using a 19th-century French tarot deck, though even a normal pack of playing cards will serve just as well to get the voices from the spirit world chattering in her head.

There are other tools of divination scattered around the room for those with eyes to see. It is said that if you gaze through the hole of a naturally-perforated stone one can see the spirit world; and the forked twisted hazel staff propped in the corner could be said to be the tool of choice for the West Country wayside witch: the 'talking stick'. As well as being a help to the wise woman in traversing hedge, moor and the old trackways, when its foot is planted on a sacred place in the landscape and its fork is placed against her brow, the wise woman may draw up the knowledge and powers of the land.

To practice the art of scrying, as well as the tools of divination and the 'witches sight' there is yet a third element to the equation that is required – you may see them sitting in the room!

The Witch's Familiars 🐾

Around the 'Wise Woman's Cottage' you can see three cats, a stoat and a perky-looking terrier dog: Blackie, Timmy, Kitty, Tosh the stoat and little Tim the dog. These all come from Cecil Williamson's collection. To the wise woman these were not only pets for companionship and pest control, they also served a magical purpose: they were the witches 'familiars'. Sadly the tale of 'little Tim the dog' has been lost, but in the museum archive there remain some of the old display labels written by Cecil Williamson (probably in the 1960s), that tell the strange and wonderful tales of the rest of the animals:

Tosh the stoat – "This stoat was a pet, familiar and gimmick of a travelling woman who made a living in the towns by reading the cards. According to the reports, 'Tosh' as he was called, picked and turned the cards and generally played an active part in the proceedings. As usual, anything highly unusual is respected and preserved. So in death, Tosh was delivered from decay. Purchased from Sandy Brown of Torrington, Devon in 1932". After seeing 'Tosh' on display in Williamson's museum in the 1950s, witchcraft expert Doreen Valiente comments: "This is in fact a correct representation of a 'divining familiar'. I have known a cat to have been used in the same way, to divine by selecting cards from an outspread pack with its paw".

Blackie the cat – "A black cat preserved for its owner who was convinced that it was her familiar. From all reports it was an unusual creature. Mrs Amy Oliver of Crewkerne (1941) worked as a 'sensitive' and made prognostications, aided by her Blackie."

Timmy the cat – "Mrs Bell of Mary Tavy, Devon, known in her lifetime as 'Fairy Bell', worshipped this cat – her beloved Timmy. Mrs Bell was a 'sensitive'; the locals of course called her a witch, she gave predictions. These she arrived at with the help of her ever-present feline spirit-force in the form of her renowned cat Timmy. In the latter part of her life she moved to Plymouth, where Timmy died in 1926. Mrs Bell saw to it that she and Timmy were not to be parted by a simple thing like death, hence this shell within which Timmy could continue an earth spirit-life with his mistress."

To understand the nature of the witch you must realise that she had one foot in this world and one foot in the spirit world. It was in the former that she primarily lived and worked but it was from the latter that she drew her power. The 'familiar' acted as a kind of messenger between these worlds; it allowed the full spirit-force to come flowing through and makes her spells work. A witch could not be a witch without a familiar, and in the days of the witch persecutions the mere possession of a pet could be enough to send you to the gallows.

Anyway, here they are today for all to see, comfortable in their native environment of the 'Wise Woman's Cottage'. The only thing they have to worry about nowadays is Tom the museum dog, who does seem to be rather interested in them!

Charms, Amulets & Tools of the Trade ॐ
Around the 'Wise Woman's Cottage' you will see a variety of weird and wonderful objects. To Old Joan however they were the everyday tools of her trade.

On the door is one of the most common magical charms which can still be seen in many places today: the *Horseshoe*. An old horseshoe, preferably one that has been found, nailed horns upwards over the door, not only attracts good luck but also keeps evil powers away. Some say it is the iron in it that gives it its 'virtue', for iron is said to repel Otherworldly forces, while others say it is calling on the powers of the mythical first blacksmith, who is also the patron of the magical artes. However, if you put one up over your door, don't forget to turn it upside-down every now and then to empty out the good luck you have collected! In the mid-17th century the antiquarian John Aubrey wrote: "It is a thing very common to nail horseshoes on to the thresholds of doors, which is to hinder the powers of witches to enter the house. Most houses in the West End of London have horseshoes on the threshold. It should be a horseshoe that one finds. In Bermuda they put an iron into the fire when a witch comes in. Mars is the enemy of Saturn".

Another charm you may see inside, that was once as popular as the horseshoe, is the *'Hagstone'*. These are naturally-holed flint stones that have been drilled through by the power of the sea. To find one was often held to be an omen of blessing from the spirit world. Hung up in the house or round the neck they attract good and kept ill at bay. Most commonly they were hung in barns to keep the fairy folk or the 'night hag' from riding the horses at night and leaving them lame and feverish in the morning, and not so long ago no fishing boat would even set sail without a 'lucky stone' fixed to its bow. These stones only occur in special places. In Cornwall they are extremely rare and presumably the witches of Devon and Dorset would have imported them for the use of their brothers and sisters in the arte in the far West. Cecil Williamson describes another use by the wayside witches for one of these strange objects: "A large heavy, single-holed flint stone, used in weather-making magic. Thread a strong, short length of cord through the hole and secure tightly. Twirl the stone as fast as one can at arm's length, around and around and listen to the whirring sound. Adjust pitch to taste".

As the founder of the museum once said: "As your car needs a garage, so you also need somewhere to keep your spirits". Around the 'Wise Woman's Cottage' you will see a number of *'spirit-houses'*: an assortment of jars, including a jar full of shells and a raggy wreath. As birds flock to a tree at sunset so the spirits roost in their little homes. He also warns:

"The thinking behind such a fabrication is complicated to say the least, and calls for a deal of folklore knowledge and an understanding of the world of spirit-force. My advice, leave well alone, just smile and say 'all rather quaint isn't it?' and then move on". Look around the cottage; how many can you see?

You will also see a *wreath of conkers*, a *wreath of apples* and a *wreath of eggs*: charms for Autumn, Halloween and Spring respectively. A necklace of *Rowan berries* gives strong protection, the *dried lemon* stuck with pins brings good luck and the *dried chillies* absorb and neutralise negativity. The *pin cushion* on the table is a spell in progress; the witch's intention is written on the cushion, then drawing on the spirit-force the pins are pushed in, whereas the labyrinth *charm bag* holds a readymade spell. Cecil Williamson comments: "Some witches' charms are just drawstring pouches with things stuffed inside. These are safe enough for a peep, but leave the sealed-up ones well alone. Always remember that". These examples were said to have come from a coven in mid-Devon that was rumoured to still be in operation in the mid 1990s.

At the back of the room you will spy an old *knotted rope*. The sea-witches that once haunted Boscastle harbour would 'tie the wind' in to knotted chords and sell them to the sailors so that they could release the them at an appropriate time. On an old display label Cecil Williamson tells: "There were well-known sea-witches selling the wind in each of the following places: Sennen, St Ives, Appledore, Lee, Lynton and Porlock, where one found Mother Leakey still trying to flog her wind-strings with their knots, right up to the mid-1930s". The rope could also be used for the casting of spells or even for making the infamous *'witch's ladder'* which is like the shaman's pole; the wayside witch could use it as a ladder and shimmy up into the spirit world. There is a famous example of one, found in an old cottage in Somerset, and now displayed in the Pitt Rivers Museum in Oxford.

What could be more typical of our image of the witch than the *cauldron* and the *broomstick*? The cauldrons displayed

here are from the Cecil Williamson
collection. Of course the cauldron was a
standard piece of kitchen equipment for
the 19th-century cook, but in the hands
of the wise woman it could be used for
the preparation of herbal potions, it could
bring spells to the boil and could even
be used to scry the mysteries. It is the
very epitome of the powers to nourish
and transform which are inherent in the
witches' arte.

On an old display label from the
museum's archive, Cecil Williamson
gives the following description: "For
the working of her witchcraft the West
Country witch depends on four main
items. First and foremost the acquisition
of a friendly and helpful familiar spirit,
second her cauldron, third her wand and
fourth her broomstick. The cauldron
is of major importance for with it the
witch is able to conjure up all manner
of spirits, such as the spirit of water in
the steam clouds: the thousand and one
odours from the sweet-smelling to the
stench of decay. The act of baking and
stewing transforms material things from

one state to another. The uses to which a witch can set her cauldron are without number; evidence for proof of the witch's constant usage of the cauldron is not far to seek, for almost every picture from bygone times depicting witchcraft activity shows a witch working near, around or over a cauldron. A witch cannot be seen without one".

The *broomstick* was also an everyday household item – a 19th-century version of the vacuum cleaner. But once again, in the hands of the witch it became a tool by which she could not only dispel unwanted influences and create a magic circle for her workings, it was also a vehicle by which she could journey to the witches' Sabbat.

Magical Herbs

"Roots of hemlock digg'd in the dusk, Slips of yew slivered in the moon's eclipse." Around the 'Wise Woman's Cottage' you will see a great assortment of *herbs*. Some came from the Williamson collection and some from the mid-Devon coven. The 'Apothecary Box' was an installation by the Truro-based artist Freyja Taylor in 2013.

As well as having a number of well-attested healing properties (indeed many of our so-called 'conventional' medicines are derived from the same herbs that the old Aunty Mays dispensed) these herbs were also the raw material for much of her spellcraft. Far from being considered 'quacks' or outsiders, many held the cunning folk in high regard as healers. Speaking of the 'white witches', the Devon folklorist Sabine Baring-Gould at the beginning of the last century stated: "That they believe in the powers and cures is true in a good number of cases, and I quite admit that they may be in possession of a large number of herbal recipes, doubtless of real efficacy. Some of our surgeons are far too fond of using the knife, and the majority of them employ strong mineral medicines that, though they may produce immediate effect, do injury in the long run".

The herbs would be gathered at a time and place appropriate to their different properties: some at sunrise and some in the dead of night, some from a spring or the north side of a hedge and some from beneath a gallows. Each of the herbs was said to be ruled by a particular planet, in the same way that astrologers say that we too are ruled. Until recently this was a mainstay of herbalism.

The planets determined what herb should be used, at what time it should be gathered and the way in which it should be used. For example, dark and poisonous herbs like hemlock or yew were said to be ruled by Saturn, while hot and prickly plants like nettle or thistle were said to be ruled by Mars. The former would be gathered at midnight in a graveyard and used for darker magical purposes, whereas the latter would be picked at sunrise on an old battlefield and used for a spell that needed a little 'Oomph'! It was even better if a horoscope was cast or an almanac of planetary hours consulted to give the exact and most potent time for harvesting and use, though without the use of books and tables, her familiar spirit and divinatory skills could often furnish the wayside witch with all the information she needed.

To ward off the 'Evil Eye', garlic, dill or St John's wort were often used; to aid one in the arts of scrying, bay, yarrow or mugwort could be employed. For healing, comfrey and meadowsweet reign supreme, and for the arts of love what better than vervain, rose and apple. You may also spy a mandrake; now that is an herb in a league of its own. It is a familiar spirit, a spirit-house, a herb and a magical tool all rolled in to one. In fact it is a thing so powerful, that it is definitely a herb that is best left for the experts!

The museum once housed a collection of 72 (a number that may be of significance to those with a familiarity with medieval magic) magical herbs in glass-fronted boxes from the Cecil Williamson collection. Sadly these were destroyed in the 2004 flood, but these few examples in the 'Wise Woman's Cottage' will give you some idea of what was used.

Two of the Original Texts Describing the 'Wise Woman's Cottage' Display 🍃

The Village Wise Woman

"She saw you into the world and she saw you out at the other end… it was just the thing you called for."

Every village in the country had a wise woman or handy woman. These women were healers, midwives, undertakers, magic-makers and fortune-tellers. They often lived in a small cottage on the outskirts of the village and would have one or more animal companions, called 'familiars'. Joan, our wise woman, is scrying (reading the future) with an old glass fishing float; these work just as well as expensive crystal balls.

Notice the various herbs and other tools of the trade. The spells that Joan speaks are traditional and collected locally. Many are still in use by witches today.

Please don't be frightened by the witches – most are like Joan and believe in helping, healing and harming none.

"MERRY MEET, MERRY PART AND MERRY MEET AGAIN!"

(The museum label outside the 'Wise Woman's Cottage' (1997) by Graham King, proprietor of the Museum of Witchcraft and Magic from 1996-2013.)

The Wise Woman

The village wise woman or cunning man used magic and wisdom to solve day-to-day problems in the village. In Cornwall they were sometimes known as pellers or pellars; today we would call them witches.

These remarkable people were known for their ability to remove curses, heal people, pets and stock and provide love potions etc. Most however specialised in a particular aspect of the craft.

"She had no fancy or expensive tools; she works with everyday objects and with what she gathers from the garden, the hedgerows and the moors, and off the seashore."

The tableau in the museum shows a village wise woman of the late-19th century. Around her are herbs, charms and tools of her trade, all of which are genuine. The soundtrack is a compilation of traditional spells and charms.

"They were consulted, not only with regard to the fortunes of those whose exact time of coming to light (the time of birth was then carefully registered, even to the minute, to serve as data on which to consult the horoscope), but were relied on for raising the spells of witchcraft, and often by their hints, advice or threats of exposure procured the restoration of stolen property. They were generally believed to have the same faculty of divination as is now assumed by the Pellar of Redruth, who is making a fortune out of the credulity of people in our enlightened times." William Bottrell (1880)
(*Commentary on the 'Wise Woman's Cottage' by Graham King, in the original 2001 Museum of Witchcraft guide book.*)

SMALLISH. STUDY.

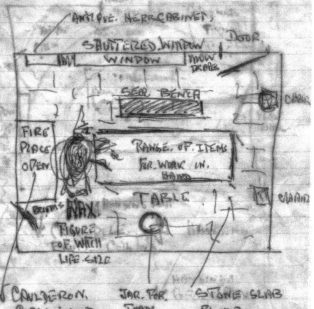

ANTIQVE. HERB CABINET;

SHUTTERED. WINDOW   DOOR.
WINDOW   WDW
                      DROPS

SEAT. BENCH   CHAIR

FIRE   RANGE. OF. ITEMS
PLACE   FOR. WORK. IN.
OPEN   HAND

                              CHAIR
BROOMS MAX.   TABLE

FIGURE
OF. WITCH
LIFE. SIZE

CAULDRON.   JAR. FOR.   STONE. SLAB
COALS. WOOD   TOADS.   FLOUR
PITCHERS CROCKS
POT HOOKS etc.   BUNCHES . OF. DRIED
                   HERBS. HANG. FROM
                   BEAMS etc.

WITCHCRAFT, THE WISE WOMAN'S COTTAGE & WEST COUNTRY CUNNING

The Museum of Witchcraft & Magic

The Museum of Witchcraft and Magic in Boscastle, Cornwall has a long and fascinating history. It began life in an old garage in Stratford-on–Avon in the late 1940s. It then journeyed onwards through a number of locations, including the now-legendary witchcraft museum on the Isle of Man in the early 1950s, Windsor and Bourton-on-the-Water in the Cotswolds, until it eventually landed in Boscastle in 1960 where it remains to this day.

It was said that it was the tales of the old sea-witches, who sold their charms and spells upon the quayside of Boscastle harbour, that initially attracted Cecil Williamson to situate his museum in Boscastle and one cannot help but feel that the magic of the sea-witches still permeates the stones of the building.

Cecil Hugh Williamson (1909-1999) was an intriguing gentleman who had a colourful career which included working on a tobacco plantation in Zimbabwe, working as a film-maker and as a spy for the British Secret Service. Throughout his life he had a deep interest in witchcraft, which began in his childhood with a number of chance encounters with the world of magic. As a result of this he devoted himself to the study of what he termed 'the silent world of witchcraft' for a period that spanned the best part of the 20th century.

He had little time, however, for what he considered to be the modern trends of occultism and paganism that were emerging at that time. His area of interest was the traditional old-time witches and cunning folk, whom he described as the 'Aunty Mays' or 'wayside witches'. It was from these that he gleaned the knowledge that provided the foundation for the museum you see today.

On All Hallows' Eve in 1996, the Museum of Witchcraft and Magic passed into the hands of folksinger and businessman Graham King, who consolidated the infrastructure of the museum and developed a library as a learning resource; he had a keen interest in representing both contemporary paganism and the folkloric element of the collection. On All Hallows' Eve 2013 the museum was once again passed on, this time to Simon Costin, director of the Museum of British Folklore. And so the story continues…

The 'Wise Woman's Cottage' ॐ

The granite building that houses the Museum of Witchcraft and Magic is a remnant of a once-thriving maritime industry that flourished in Boscastle. In the past it has been variously a fish-cellar, a smoke-house and a warehouse, but now the labyrinthine twists and turns of its rooms and corridors within, and the numinous brooding splendour of the valley without make a perfect setting for a journey into the twilight world of witchcraft.

In passing through the doors of the museum, one continues through the 'outer court', presided over by the wishing well. Then one passes through the first two chambers until a sharp bend brings you in to what seems to be the very heart of the museum – the 'Wise Woman's Cottage'. It is fitting in a way that a tableau such as this should occupy the museum's centre, for it was upon the words and the ways of the 'Aunty Mays' and the wayside witches that the museum was indeed built.

The Tableaux of the Museum:
A 'Geek' into the Otherworld 🕷

The Museum of Witchcraft and Magic has a tradition going back to its earliest days of the use of tableaux. Cecil Williamson often referred to the museum as being his 'spider's web' in that it attracted both a source of financial income and the even more valuable fragments of half-forgotten witch lore that interested parties brought to his door. He was also known to describe himself as a 'showman', and to him the sticky heart of this 'spider's web' was his tableaux. To the passing tourists they could be good old-fashioned spooky entertainment, but maybe to those with a little knowledge they were a bit more.

Up until the 1990s, the museum at Boscastle housed three tableaux as part of its display: the 'Temple of Tanat', the 'Horned God' and the 'Witches' Cradle'. These bizarrely idiosyncratic tableaux seemed to be unconnected with any contemporary ideas of paganism and magical practice. They were dark and challenging and some considered them to be little more than a lurid and tasteless peepshow for the tourists, though Cecil Williamson himself hinted that they were a genuine representation of a hidden witch tradition in the West Country.

When Graham King took over the museum in 1996, he came in with a clean sweep from a new witch's besom! Structurally little work had been done on the museum for some years and it was in need of a significant amount of maintenance. He also wished to reinterpret the collection in a way more in accordance with contemporary ideas of museum displays. Consequently the layout of the museum was completely redesigned. In the process the three old tableaux were dismantled and two new tableaux came into being: the 'Stone Circle' (which in 2013 was dismantled and replaced by the new exhibition space) and the 'Wise Woman's Cottage'.

The 'Wise Woman's Cottage' Past & Present ⚜

In the 1951 guide book to the Isle of Man museum, Cecil Williamson also announces that in addition to his existing displays he had in preparation a display of "a typical 17th century witch's kitchen with a room set ready for the working of magic etc". It is unclear whether this was ever built as no images or records of it remain. In 1954, in Gerald Gardner's subsequent museum 'The Witches' Mill', there was a tableau of a witch casting a spell (with a bizarrely-anachronistic floral bedspread in the background!). It is unlikely that this was Williamson's work. However, in 1956 in Williamson's

Bourton-on-the-Water museum in the Cotswolds, the tableau seems to have been constructed. Again, no images have been found but a sketch of the ground plan remains in the museum archive which, interestingly, appears to be remarkably similar to the display currently in the Boscastle museum.

In Doreen Valiente's *ABC of Witchcraft Past and Present* (1973) there is a description of the Bourton-on-the-Water museum. She recalled that in addition to the controversial 'Temple of Tanat' (which was one of the three tableaux that Williamson had in the subsequent Boscastle museum) there was also housed "a life-sized representation of a scene of an old-time witch's cottage, showing how a 'divining familiar' worked".

She goes on to describe a rather Gothic and 'Williamson-esque' interpretation of the witch's cottage: "A wax figure of a witch sat before a big old-fashioned table, on which was a skull draped in a black shawl; also on the table were a black-hilted knife, and four candles in crude homemade candlesticks of bone.

79

Specimens of herbs were displayed before the familiar, a small animal (a weasel, I think). It was explained that the animal became possessed with a god or a spirit, and indicated the right herb to use in a particular case".

The 'small animal' in question is of course 'Tosh' the stoat, who inhabits the present-day 'Wise Woman's Cottage' display.

In the 1990s the witch's cottage once again emerged in the Boscastle museum. At the time Graham King had no idea that there had previously been a witch's cottage in Williamson's museums, let alone the similarity of its layout, but as Mr King wryly remarked: "There are rarely any new ideas in the Museum of Witchcraft; Cecil has always done it before!". Cecil Williamson insisted that the spirits were always looking over the museum, so should we be surprised at synchronicities such as this? Mr King explained: "I saw the cottage as a chance to demonstrate a lot of folk-magic charms in an entertaining way; it also serves to replace the dated and tacky tableaux".

Familliar spirit animals of 'The Wise Woman's Cottage'

Facing: Painted egg shell and 'conker' charms hung from the beams of the cottage.

Above: Pin-cushion heart charm.

Right: A rope of magical knots on the wise woman's table.

Top: A raggy wreath charm from a Devon coven, and the alcove set with a carved slate from the Cecil Williamson collection. Above: 'Old Joan' with the tools of her tade.

In the spring of 1998, on the site of the old 'Witches' Cradle' tableau, Graham King and his then-partner Liz Crow, a team of volunteers and some local builders constructed the 'Wise Woman's Cottage'. The granite lintel over the fireplace was provided by the St Just-based sculptor Rory Te 'Tigo and much of the contents were both provided and sponsored by a witches' coven from mid-Devon.

Once again this was constructed in accordance with the way in which Graham King wished to represent witchcraft and his vision for the museum. He chose to neither represent the witch as an oppressed victim nor as being a sinister or macabre caricature, as so many representations seem to be. He portrayed her as an independent woman, learned in her artes and part of her community. This presented what many would consider to be a more traditional, historical representation of a 19th-century cunning woman. One can detect a nod towards the wise women represented in the folklore record of the West Country, such as Anne Jefferies,

Tamsin Blight, Cherry of Morwenstow, or even one of Cecil Williamson's wayside witches of the 20th century.

Graham King also added another innovation: a soundtrack consisting of a litany of spells and incantations spoken over the sound of a crackling fire, being played continuously as a backdrop to the scene. This had a dual function; not only did it bring an otherwise inanimate scene to life, it also acted as a way of contextualising many of the charms and objects in the cabinets around the museum. It demonstrated that the material objects on display were only part of the story, that they only 'came to life' when used as part of a spell or spoken charm.

The charms originally used were an eclectic mix of spells and incantations, primarily from Wiccan and folkloric sources and curated by Levannah Morgan (author and founder of the 'Friends of the Museum of Witchcraft') and voiced by Cassandra Latham-Jones (author and "Witch of Buryan").

The wise woman in the tableau is a kindly-faced elderly lady, dressed in the common garb of someone of middle-income in the latter part of the 19th century. The room is a generic room rather than a reproduction of any historically specific place. She is seated at a table and around her are a number of artefacts, many of which were taken from Cecil Williamson's collection and in all probability have a genuine witchcraft pedigree. One is reminded of Cecil Williamson's own description of an old-time witch which is given earlier in this book:

"These ladies are solo workers, they do not have to seek clients, for those with problems come knocking on their door. Payment is not sought or asked for, it is given by the client, and there are no tools of the trade or regalia, no covenstead decorated with symbols or signs. Natural objects such as twigs, stones and flowers etc are sometimes used".

The figure herself was commissioned for the tableau by Graham King and was produced by a company that specialised in making museum mannequins. The mannequins in Williamson's old displays were often likened to 'shop dummies'. This was not strictly true, but they were rather standardised in appearance. Graham King however wanted a high-quality mannequin, modelled on an actual person.

Dr Margaret Murray, in her seminal work *The God of the Witches* (1931), claimed that certain names seem to reoccur time and time again in the history of witchcraft and appear to be specifically associated with the witches: the name 'Joan' was one such name. The skeleton of Joan Wytte, 'The Fighting Fairy Woman of Bodmin', who was displayed in the museum for many years, and was considered by some to be a 'patron spirit' of the place, was an example of this. So for the museum team it came as no surprise that the model on whom the mannequin was based was a lady by the name of 'Joan'. Naturally the figure became known as 'Joan' and the tableau came to be informally known as 'Joan's Cottage'.

In 2013 the new management team of the museum produced a leaflet entitled *Spells and Remedies from Joan's Cottage* which included a description of the display, a selection of the spoken charms and some magical herbal remedies. To link in with the witch's cottage display a small herb garden, known as 'Joan's Garden' was also established at the front of the museum. It was planted with magical herbs acknowledged to have been used by the cunning folk, including rosemary, angelica, parsley, St John's wort, camomile, borage and sage.

In 2015 the 'Wise Woman's Cottage' received a makeover, including a new voice-over soundtrack. The charms for this were all collected from Cornwall and Devon, some in the very locality of the museum, and were known to have been used by cunning folk in the 18th, 19th and early-20th centuries. These were curated by the author and voiced by Elaine Gill (author, actor, artist, musician and Cornish speaker who lives in Newlyn) – and there the 'Wise Woman's Cottage' still stands today!

Strange Tales! ❧

There are a number of strange tales connected with the 'Wise Woman's Cottage'. Over the years there have regularly been reports given to the museum staff by visitors of sightings of movements in Joan's mannequin; this has ranged from subtle movements in her hands, head and eyes to actual reports of her breathing!

During the construction of the tableau, all was in place and ready to go except for one thing that was missing: a large quantity of local stone was needed for the construction of the front wall of the cottage. As Graham King described: "'twas way beyond our budget". Consequently construction ground to a halt. Then, as if some unseen force had heeded their plight, within days a mighty storm blew up in the night. Graham King described it thus:

"The following night there was a huge storm and the waves were breaking against the front of the museum; we had to move our cars etc. from the car park. The following morning the car park was covered with debris including tons and tons of nicely-rounded, large stones. The National Trust was pleased to accept our offer to clear them up and, after two days and several wheelbarrows, the car park was clear and Neptune had provided us with all the building materials we needed!".

The stone was gathered, the wall was built and the day was saved.

In another strange tale the sea once more played a part in the history of the 'Wise Woman's Cottage'. On the 16th of August 2004, again severe weather conditions combined with an unusually high tide, and a devastating flood swept through Boscastle, destroying swathes of the village in its wake. Floodwaters poured through the front of the museum, inundating the entire ground floor. Despite the widespread destruction in the village, within the museum relatively little was lost or destroyed and the building remained intact. However, the carved wooden sign (made by the author) for the 'Wise Woman's Cottage' was swept out of the harbour and across the open sea in to the Atlantic for some considerable distance and was eventually found washed ashore at Monknash beach in South Wales. The sign was returned and the 'Wise Woman's Cottage' rebuilt, and all was well. One cannot help but think that the old sea-witches that once haunted the quay were still there in spirit, keeping a weather-eye on the place.

The Spells of the Wise Woman's Cottage 🗝
Within the 'Wise Woman's Cottage' you will hear a selection of actual 19th century charms and spells from the West Country being spoken.

The wayside witches were no fools when it came to the casting of spells. They would use the most effective tools and techniques at their disposal in order to achieve their 'beneficial positive results' as efficiently as possible, whether this was the use of herbs, magical signs or sigils or even household tools and implements such as candles, pots and pans or a hammer and nails.

Accordingly, around the Museum of Witchcraft and Magic you will see a whole variety of different means of working magic. All of them employ the same principle of somehow binding the intangible spirit-force of a spell into a physical form so that it could be utilised by the operator. We see examples of spells and charms written or scratched onto paper, parchment or other hard surfaces, but the written word seems to have been used in tandem with the spoken word. These spells were not static; they were enacted and brought to life and it is this process that we see represented in the 'Wise Woman's Cottage'. The use of the spoken and the written charms tended to have a strange relationship; some claimed that their 'virtue' would be destroyed and the charms would consequently be rendered useless if they were ever written down. For instance see *Footprints of Former Men in Far Cornwall* – R S Hawker (1870). However, many examples have been preserved of the use of written spells in the form of charms and talismans, and indeed many of the spoken charms in this collection apparently come from the charmers' own written notebooks.

A picture of how the spoken charms were viewed is given in this 19th-century account of cunning craft from Devon: "Warts and swellings are removed by various charms, such as skeins of thread knotted with the number of warts to be removed, and struck across the warts as many times and then buried; or striking with a wych elm wand, or a piece of stolen bacon. In each of which cases, as the buried article decays so do the warts gradually decrease; or by depositing a given number of pebbles or peas in a bag, and losing it, but in this case the unfortunate finder gets the warts himself. But the most favourite remedy for warts and indeed all swellings are to have 'words' said over them".

The use of 'words' or spoken charms is one of the core practices of the wayside witch, and fortunately a number of these have been preserved and, some say, are still in use today. Such charms and spells have a long and venerable tradition going back to the earliest forms of magic, and who could deny that there is not a certain kind of magic in the idea that an abstract and intangible thought could be locked up, preserved and even passed around in the form of an articulated sound. As to whether these words of magic are just a type of hypnosis or autosuggestion, or whether they are intrinsically magical and do indeed call upon the aid of Otherworldly powers, or are even part of some big confidence trick is a decision the reader needs to make for themselves. Spoken charms or spells take a variety of forms. They can be spoken alone or in conjunction with some ritual or magical act. Sometimes they must be spoken at a particular place or time (for example, at a crossroads at sunset, on a special holy day, or in a magical circle at a specific planetary hour) for them to be effective. There are some elaborate examples in the magical 'grimoires' or books of magic from the medieval period and some quite simple ones in the folk tradition that can be spoken repetitively, in a similar fashion to the way that 'mantras' are used in the East. However, there is one factor common to the use of all spoken charms, and that is that they are only part of a magical equation; as Cecil Williamson describes: "There are basically four parts to a magical operation (the spell or charm). First you have a source of elemental spirit-force; second you have the witch; third you have the client and fourth, the objective".

It is a common belief in many cultures that languages that are considered to be marginal and archaic have a particular magical efficacy. Maybe these so-called 'gibberish' elements to the spells are survivals of old languages such as Latin or Cornish. For example the term 'hocus pocus', often used as a parody of a magical charm, is derived from a colloquial rendering of part of the Latin Roman Catholic Mass. In Cornwall charms were sometimes referred to as 'nomnys', which also seems to be derived from the above source in the benediction *'In nomine Patris, et Filii, et Spiritus Sancti'*.

In the world of magic and folk tradition, the very definitions of what we commonly hold to be Christian or pagan tend to blur and fade like the horizon between the sky and the sea on a hazy autumn day.

The charms collected for the 'Wise Woman's Cottage' are all spoken in a recognisable form of English, though many contain an element of Cornish dialect and some also incorporate apparent 'nonsense' words; there may be more to this than is immediately evident. Cornwall has its own language; it is an ancient Celtic language similar to Breton and Welsh. The received wisdom once stated that the last-recorded native Cornish speaker was Dolly Pentreath of Mousehole in West Cornwall, who died in 1777 (and incidentally was also known to be a witch of some renown!) but now it is more generally thought that the language continued to be widely-used among the working people in Cornwall as late as the early-20th century. These charms were collected by English speakers and consequently they were given in the English language. However it is quite likely that when they were originally used, the Cornish language was employed.

You may notice that many of the spells take the form of prayers, with some incorporating the liturgical language of church and chapel, the Psalms, Biblical references, and that many finish with 'Amen' or 'In the name of the Father, the

Son and the Holy Ghost'. This raises a number of questions about the nature of these spells, not least whether they are 'Christian' or 'pagan'. The answer I fear is a complicated one and there is an ongoing debate amongst scholars on this subject. Of course it also depends on how one defines 'Christian' and 'pagan', and also as to how one defines a 'witch'!

What is a Witch? 🐾

So, I hear you ask – what is a witch? Well, there is no simple or single answer to this question. The image of the witch that we hold is a river fed by many streams.

🐾 **The Modern Witch:** In our modern times, by far the most prevalent image of witchcraft is that derived from Wicca, which is a religion founded by Gerald Gardner. He claimed that it was a modern incarnation of an ancient pagan witch-cult that survived from prehistoric times in to the modern age. He also claimed to have been initiated into this in the New Forest in the 1940s. It has become a hugely-popular worldwide religion;

Professor Ronald Hutton asserts that it is the only religion Britain has ever exported to the rest of the world.

Wicca centres on a belief in a god and a goddess, which are considered to be pre-Christian pagan deities; consequently Wicca draws heavily on pre-Christian mythology as a source of inspiration. Both the theology and the practice is organised around a cycle of annual calendar customs connected to the solstices and the equinoxes and called the 'Wheel of the Year'; many consider this to be an embodiment of their mysteries. Originally Wiccan practice was based on a sexually-charged occult ritual, but now it tends towards ceremonial, devotional, magical and healing practices, many of which are drawn from those popular in the New Age movement. Entrance into Wicca is by initiation; some work in covens although nowadays most work on their own, and many even favour the more modern social-networking media as their preferred form of gathering. Wiccan witches work their magic either in the nude ('skyclad') or in ceremonial robes.

Often they employ elaborate ceremonial jewellery and accoutrements, such as ritual swords or the 'athame' (the witch's knife). Wiccans consider themselves to be direct descendants of the witches. However, Cecil Williamson, the founder of the Museum of Witchcraft and Magic, gave a very different account of the story.

❧ Wicca & the Museum of Witchcraft & magic: The story of Wicca and the Museum of Witchcraft and Magic is a tangled skein. Cecil Williamson first met Gerald Gardner in London shortly after the war, in the late 1940s. Gardner had just returned from overseas and had an interest in Classical paganism, tribal practices, folklore, the occult, swords, flagellation and naturism. He saw witchcraft as an umbrella by which he could synthesise these into a system of practice, a new religion. Williamson too had an interest in witchcraft, but his came from his studies of folk-magic andfieldwork with traditional witches.

The two men met briefly in London and then went their separate ways.

Williamson moved to the Isle of Man and opened his museum, 'The Folklore Centre of Superstition and Witchcraft'. No sooner did Williamson have it up and running when who should turn up on his doorstep but Gardner. It appeared that he had nowhere to go and seemed to be in some kind of trouble, so Williamson took him in. He was a charming fellow so Williamson installed him in the museum café as 'the resident witch' to entertain the visitors. Gardner eventually bought a house on the island and became more seriously involved in the museum and began to develop his ideas of Wicca. After some time the relationship between the two men, for a variety of reasons, began to sour and there was an acrimonious parting of the ways. Gardner bought the building and the Isle of Man museum continued as 'The Witches' Mill' until the 1970s. Williamson took the collection and subsequently set up a series of museums in England until he, and it, eventually settled in Boscastle in 1960.

Williamson and Gardner had radically different visions of witchcraft. On one hand Gardner saw it as a ceremonially-based pagan religion for the masses, whereas Williamson saw it as a path for only the few. For him it was an operative magical system which was intrinsically connected to the spirit world, and had nothing to do with any idea of 'paganism' or what he saw to be the ostentatious rituals of Wicca. Most of all he felt that Gardner was disdainful of both magic and the old-time witches, neither of which he was interested in. However, as history reveals, Gardner 'got the gig' and Williamson disappeared into obscurity. The reason for this is, in my mind, quite evident; both men got what they wanted. Gardner got his popular religion and Williamson retired with his underground, chthonic, Otherworldly wayside witchery. But in his writings Williamson barely disguises his frustration at the flowering of the 'new-fangled' Wicca, which he saw as bearing no relation to the witchcraft he had encountered amongst the folk practitioners and the wayside witches.

Consequently, Cecil Williamson was quite dismissive of Wicca in the early days of the museum. Over the years this has changed. In the 1990s Graham King incorporated many Wiccan and neo-pagan elements into the museum (along with many other contemporary magical practices) in order to be more representative of modern magical beliefs. Simon Costin has continued this trend and has developed the folklore theme as a key element in the continuing story.

Wicca has gained enormous popularity and, as even Cecil Williamson conceded, it has bought "joy, happiness, peace of mind and self-understanding to so many people". However, in terms of the study of magical traditions some may consider that one of the more problematic aspects of Wicca is that it has become a victim of its own success and has become the lens through which we now see all witchcraft. So many aspects of traditional folk-magic have been rejected and sidelined purely because they do not fit in with the Wiccan hegemony. The Museum of Witchcraft and Magic has long been a victim of this. It portrayed a world of magic born of moors and the wild sea, where the shadowy figure of the wayside witch brooded 'twixt this world and the shadowy spirit world – an aspect of magical belief that Cecil Williamson claimed was the bread-and-butter of the ordinary working people of Britain.

So, this still begs the question: where did the Wiccans, and indeed many others in the 19th and 20th centuries, derive their image of the witch from?

❦ **The Medieval Witch:** Our image of witchcraft in many ways has been formed by the baroque and florid medieval accounts of witchcraft that came from the European mainland, especially France and Germany. Here we have tales of the witch on her broomstick, sweeping effortlessly between the romantic and the grotesque as she flies across the night sky to the witches' Sabbat, there to indulge herself in the diabolical delights of the blasphemous orgiastic feast before her lord and master – the Devil himself! These images have been immortalised as far back as the 15th century in the illustrations of Durer, Grien, Meilich and

Veneziano among others (many of which Williamson displayed in the museum).

The persecutions of the witches were equally overblown: a plague of imprisonments, torture and execution by burning, instigated by the Church and the Inquisition, swept across Roman Catholic Europe on a monumental scale. The persecutors proclaimed that: "There is never a witch alone". They were seen to be part of a kind of a satanic 'anti-Church', an organised 'fifth column' hidden within our communities seeking to overthrow the Church, the state and even God himself. The story of witchcraft in Britain was however a much more staid affair.

In the British Isles there were still tales of 'shapeshifting' and magic, and of course there was still persecution of the witches, but the exotic tales of the Sabbat were all but absent, being replaced by tales of imps and familiars who came to the witches as they tarried in the lonely places, to aid them in their revels of a far more domestic nature. The persecutions in Britain were a civil matter dealt with by the courts. Torture was, for the most part, illegal and there were no burnings at the stake. Witchcraft was treated as a crime like sheep stealing or murder, and execution, when it was implemented, was by the noose.

❧ 18th, 19th & 20th Century Witches: The 17th century heralded the beginning of the modern world. Out of the chaos of a land torn apart by civil war came a host of new ideas and new ways of thinking, including a move away from the mysticism inherent in Roman Catholicism and towards ideas of rationality and reason. Also, in many ways it marked a watershed in how people perceived witchcraft In 1682 in Exeter in Devon, the last witch in Britain was officially executed.

By the end of the 17th century, the bloody persecutions of the Medieval and Tudor periods, whether they were by gallows, stake, prison or torture chamber, seem to have run their course. In recent times the blame for the perpetration of these atrocities is mostly laid upon the Church. However, the mainstream

Church tends to blame Christian sects, or even the Rationalists and the emerging legal profession, while the Rationalists blame the 'mob' whipped up with group hysteria. We shall never know the full story of what happened, but whether it was nine hundred or nine million who died, it was a terrible tragedy of human history that should never have happened.

The witch persecutions in Europe may have burned out but in West Africa and Nigeria a witch persecution on a scale similar to anything we saw in the European Middle Ages is, at the time of writing, still in full swing. A special unit has been set up in London, which in 2015 investigated over 60 incidents.

The arrival of the 18th century was by no means the end of either the belief in witchcraft, or the persecution of witches. Although the mainstream Protestant church tended to shy away from any ideas of the supernatural, the idea of the tangible agency of spiritual forces at work on the earth was eagerly embraced by many of the Puritan and Non-Conformist sects, including Methodism, so popular in the western counties of England. Hand-in-hand with this went the belief in witchcraft. In the mid-19th century the Reverend Stephen Hawker exclaimed:

"Two-thirds of the total population of Tamarside (Devon and Cornwall) implicitly believe in the power of *Mal Occhio*, as the Italians name it, or the Evil Eye".

The image of the witch, however, began to change. They came to be defined not in terms of their persecution, but more in terms of the magical role they had in the community and we see the growth of what has come to be known as the 'cunning traditions' – 'cunning' being an archaic word for skilled or wise (although, ironically, the term 'cunning' from its very beginning carried its present-day connotation). The old cunning folk seem to have been regarded in equal measure as both skilled in magic and as charlatans. Behind closed doors those who worked the Ritual High Magical practices of the 'grimoires' (the mediaeval magical texts) and the puffings of the alchemists, continued to wend their way towards their 'Great Work'. Although their names and roles often overlap, the public practice of the magical artes (which I believe to be a defining feature of the cunning tradition) could be said to fall roughly into four camps.

First, there were the healers or 'charmers'. They would practice either hands-on or distant forms of healing. Sometimes they would employ charms or prayers such as those spoken in the 'Wise Woman's Cottage'. Often they would specialise in a particular ailment such as ringworm, toothache or blood staunching. Their ability was considered a gift, passed on from family or other healers, though ultimately it was thought to be of divine origin. They rarely charged for their services and they were hardly ever persecuted. There is a number of this type of charmer still working in North Cornwall today.

Second, there were the 'ghost-layers' or what we would now call, exorcists. They seem to have been universally male and were frequently drawn from the ranks of the upper class, often the clergy. They were educated and literate and regularly employed elaborate ceremonial, magical techniques and they specialised in the laying of spirits to rest. Well-documented examples of these in Cornwall in the 18th and 19th century were Parson Woods of Ladock, the Reverend Richard Doidge of Talland and the Reverend Mr Polkinhorne of St Ives. One must be aware that post-Reformation, within the Protestant churches the party line was that ghosts did not exist. Paradoxically this meant that no means of dealing with them was provided if or when a ghost did arise! One could argue that the cunning practitioners, and especially the ghost-layers, emerged to fill the gap left by the ousted Roman Catholic priests.

Third, there were the fortune-tellers. They worked professionally, often travelling from farm to farm or stopping at country fairs. They used the cards, the crystal ball or any number of other ingenious devices (some of which are shown in the Museum of Witchcraft and Magic, such as Bessie Brook's divination mat or Kate 'the Gull' Turner's tambourine). The Romany travellers were famed for their skills in this area; often non-Romany fortune-tellers would claim Romany ancestry in order to gain kudos in this field.

Fourth, there were the 'conjurors' or cunning folk, called in the South West of Britain 'white witches' or 'pellers'. Peller is a name of uncertain origin, possibly either from the Cornish 'pellhe' (to drive away) or a shortening of the English 'expeller' or 'peddler'. These people were somewhat closer to our traditional view of the witch and practised a mixed bag of magical artes; both men and women worked their artes professionally. They used divination for the finding of lost or stolen goods, or to discover the perpetrators of malefic magic. They also made charms for the making or breaking of spells, both for good or ill, depending on the inclination of the peller or the payment from the client! Some were persecuted, some were valued members of the community, and some (like Tamsin Blight of Helston) even worked from professional consulting rooms in the centres of well-to-do Cornish market towns. A few became famous in their own lifetimes, though most just quietly worked their magical artes within their communities.

Where they got there magical skills from is another question. Some of them would have had their knowledge or 'virtue' passed down within their family or professional lineages; some seemed to have studied the magical texts, of which there were many by the 19th century, though Cecil Williamson clearly stated that the core of the witch's power lay in the fact that she was in possession of a spirit familiar, which in turn gave her access to the spirit world and the powers it bestows.

It is from this latter category that Cecil Williamson drew much of his knowledge. He called them the wayside witches, the sea-witches or 'Aunty Mays' (the latter because if you ask them for help, Aunty 'may' or 'may not'!). It is upon one such as this that Old Joan in the 'Wise Woman's Cottage' is based.

FOUR WEST COUNTRY WITCHES

The 'droll-tellers' of old spoke of the witches of legend who could fly upon their ragwort stalks (unlike their 'broomstick-riding' up-country cousins!) to gather at their great midsummer Sabbats on the moors above Zennor or on the cliffs of St Levan, in the far west of Cornwall. But to find the kind of peller who would inhabit our own 'Wise Woman's Cottage' we need to look for a witch of a far more corporeal nature. Luckily the folkloric records have preserved some fascinating tales of the cunning folk who once roamed abroad in this land. As you will see, however, history is a fickle friend, and where myth, stories and faithful accounts merge into one another is never entirely clear. As you may have already gathered, in the world of magic things are rarely as they seem, and so often what we firmly hold to be facts, on closer inspection begin to shimmer and melt like the morning mist. So here are the tales of four West Country witches, which will hopefully give you a glimpse in to the 'silent world of witchcraft'.

Joan Wytte

From the museum's arrival in Boscastle in 1960, one of Cecil Williamson's prime exhibits was the skeleton of Joan Wytte, known as 'The Fighting Fairy Woman of Bodmin'. To many people she has become an almost totemic spirit presiding over the museum, though ironically almost nothing is actually known about her. With the centripetal pull that any mystery creates, a host of myths has gathered around her and she has become many things to many people: to some a persecuted witch, to others a wise healer – and to some a complete fiction!

Shortly after Graham King took over the museum in the mid-1990s, there commenced an enigmatic tale. She remained on display in the museum for just over a year. In this time a number of ghostly events were witnessed around the skeleton, one of which was observed by the author – but that is another story! Then, out of the blue, Williamson's prize exhibit was taken out of the display and placed under the new proprietor's bed for some months. At about the same time that the 'Wise Woman's Cottage' was under construction, on a dark and stormy night on the dark of the moon in October 1998, Graham King and two friends took the skeleton of Joan Wytte up to Minster woods and gave her a 'decent' burial. Now even her mortal remains are gone; all we have is Cecil Williamson's tale and the memory of her bones.

The original text by Cecil Williamson mainly tells of her background. He explains that she was born in Bodmin in 1775 and died of bronchial pneumonia in Bodmin Gaol in 1813. She was originally a weaver and yarn-twister by trade before working as a 'tawer' or white leather worker. He claims that the skeleton was inspected by a Home Office forensic expert, who determined that her bones were rich in kaolin and natural fluoride, which would tally with her place of residence and her occupation. He also pointed out that she had evidence of a huge abscess in her tooth, which would have caused her great pain and possibly account for her violent behaviour, which in turn may have led to her incarceration. Regarding her being a witch, all we have is the presence of 'Fairy' in her name and a reference to her as being 'The Bodmin Witch' in Williamson's notes. After this the trail begins to disappear.

Some of the names and events in Williamson's account can be corroborated, but records are few and sparse in content and much remains unknown. At this point the story far from ends as Joan began to develop a whole host of new stories, not just tales of her life but also those regarding her authenticity. For example, in addition to the original anonymous Home Office forensic report, there appeared stories of another report in which she is described as not being a single person, but rather a composite skeleton constructed from odds and ends, for teaching purposes.

In 1999 Kelvin Jones, in his book *Seven Cornish Witches*, elaborates on Cecil's story. From her connection to Scarlett Well (mentioned in Williamson's notes) and its folkloric healing powers, he develops the theme of her being a healer. He also relates how Williamson actually acquired the skeleton and tells how, after she died in gaol, Joan's body was used as a skeleton for teaching medical students. As a prank it was once used in a séance, which culminated in violent poltergeist activity. It was then passed on to a doctor in North Cornwall, and then to the antique dealer who sold her to Cecil Williamson.

Also in the 1990s the anthropologist Dr Helen Cornish began a study on Joan

Wytte (which is still in progress today) and the ways in which the story has grown within the pagan community; thus Joan began a new journey into the world of academia. In 2003 the folklorist, singer and story-teller Kathy Wallace wrote and performed a play about Joan Wytte. In this she emphasised her role as a persecuted herbalist, healer and proto-feminist witch. From this point on her role was set. Still today she is by considered many, without question, to have been a genuine Cornish witch, and every year in autumn there is a pilgrimage from the museum to her grave in the woods.

Sometimes, as the evenings draw in and the museum is quiet, one is led to muse on the idea that when her skeleton left the building her presence came to rest in the 'Wise Woman's Cottage'. Even though her mortal remains have been laid to rest, her story still stands firm before the viewing public. For the moment, the question as to whether she is a monument to our credulity or to our empathy must remain unresolved.

MARIANN VOADEN, BRATTON

Mariann Voaden 🐝

The Devon folklorist Sabine Baring-Gould in his 1908 work *Devonshire Characters and Strange Events* recalled the life of a witch by the name of Mariann Voaden whom he encountered at Bratton Clovelly in north Devon. He describes her thus:

"She was esteemed as a witch – a white one of course. She was a God-fearing woman and had no relations with the Evil One, of that one may be sure. How she subsisted was a puzzle to the whole parish. But, then, she was generally feared; she received presents from every farm and cottage".

He portrays her, as is the fashion with many of the old cunning folk, as being both trickster and healer. As well as running a kind of 'protection racket' terrorising the local children, she was a renowned healer and blood stauncher. Baring-Gould tells of how she affected distant cures by the blessing of folk's handkerchiefs, and that it was not uncommon to see the postman arriving at her hovel holding a kerchief at arm's length, sent from some ailing fellow to be blessed.

Perhaps, most interestingly, she was in possession of a notebook of charms, spells and recipes. Baring-Gould managed to record a number of them, including charms for whooping cough, scalds, sprain, blood staunching and toothache, and an ointment for sprains (which includes in its ingredients earthworms and Spanish Fly!). Indeed some of these appear in this volume in the Litany of Spells spoken in the 'Wise Woman's Cottage'.

In his book, Baring-Gould reproduces a quite remarkable photograph of Mariann Voaden standing at the cave-like door of her decaying cob and thatch cottage, looking every inch the village wise woman. He goes on to say:

"She must have been handsome in her day, with a finely-cut profile and piercing dark eyes. She usually wore a red kerchief about her head and a red petticoat. But she was dirty – indescribably so. Her hands were the colour of mahogany".

She seemed to live in extraordinary squalor and her house was quite literally falling down around her. Despite all protestation from her neighbours she steadfastly refused any offers of help to repair it, even when offered for free or in exchange for a blessing. To the thatcher she said: "God made the sky, and that is the best roof of all", and to the rector: "There be two angels that sit on the rungs of that ladder and watches there, that nobody comes nigh me, and that they be ready to hold up the timbers that they don't fall on me". Eventually gravity and entropy had their way. Whilst being reduced to living under a makeshift lean-to at one end of the house, her small cooking fire ignited the remains of her house, destroying all she had, including her book of charms. Baring-Gould relates that she spent the last of her days in the relative comfort of the workhouse.

This brief sketch of the white witch Mariann Voaden throws a number of our preconceptions about the cunning folk up into the air. She was a God-fearing well-loved member of the community. Although poor, she was literate and independent. She appeared to be in possession of very real powers and her odd behaviour can only be explained by her displaying a kind of stoic mysticism worthy of Diogenes, a Zen master or some eastern sadhu! An old West Country witch once said to Cecil Williamson: "To understand the world you must stand on your head" and one cannot help but ponder that these words may have come from old Mariann Voaden herself.

Cherry of Morwenstow 🐝

In the Museum of Witchcraft and Magic there stands a rather unassuming pestle and mortar, but beneath it the inscription reads: "This old turned-wood witch's mortar and pestle is reputed to have been used by Charity West,

Mortar and Pestle
This old turned wood witch's mortar and pestle is reputed to have been used by Charity West, better known as Old Cherry of Welcombe, Morwenstow.

better known as Old Cherry of Welcombe, Morwenstow".

Much of what we know of this enigmatic dame comes from the writings of a most incredible character: the priest, poet, mystic and folklorist, the Reverend Robert Stephen Hawker (1803-1875). He was the vicar of the parish of Morwenstow, on the Cornwall-Devon border, some 15 miles up the coast from the museum in Boscastle. It is a wild and isolated place, bounded by murderous cliffs, washed by the Atlantic on one side and with impenetrable moorland on the inland approach. Within his charge was an even more isolated place: a hamlet of some 200 souls, cut off by land and water, by the name of Welcombe (which he writes about under the name of 'Holacombe'). Baring-Gould in his 1913 biography of Hawker describes its inhabitants as: "People of a different race of those in adjoining parishes, with black eyes and hair, and dark-skinned ('dark-grained as a Welcombe woman' is a saying in the neighbourhood) who held faith in both God and the world of spirits in equal measure. One such member of this hamlet was a witch by the name of Old Cherry".

Of the fact that Old Cherry was a witch, the Reverend Hawker was in no doubt. He states: "I have seen the five black spots placed diagonally under her tongue, which are evidence of what she is. They are like those in the feet of swine, made by the entrance in to them of the demons at Gadara". He relates a tale of how Cherry came to his door begging for skimmed milk, of which he had none. On leaving his house she muttered something over the pigsty. From that moment onwards the sow turned, like 'Medea' upon her own piglets, and one by one they died. The 'Evil Eye' had surely been cast upon them! In another tale Old Cherry went to a local farmer begging for wood and after a polite refusal she once again turned away muttering. That night a violent and destructive storm swept across the parish. The disgruntled farmer marched up to Hawker protesting that after faithfully paying his tithes and rates all these years: "I do not think that ones such as Old Cherry Parnell never ought to be allowed to meddle in such things as thunder and lightning".

In yet another tale, another farmer approached Hawker claiming that Old Cherry had stolen his hen. "The Vicar had his cross-handled walking stick in his hand, a sort of oriental pastoral staff; he forthwith drew a circle in the dust and sketched a pentacle within it – Solomon's seal." He then pronounced that the hen had not left the lane, and sure enough, satisfied that the powers of Old Cherry were nullified, the farmer found the errant hen in his lane.

As to her life, once again little is known. C. E. Byles, direct descendant and biographer of Hawker, suggests in his 1905 work that Charity/Cherry West/Parnell may be a pseudonym for Sally Found, an inhabitant of the parish who was also credited with the ability to 'ill wish'. These tales of Old Cherry as a dark, destructive elemental force may however only just be part of the story. As Baring-Gould states of Hawker: "Living as he did in a visionary dream-world of spirits, he was ready to admit, without questioning, the stories he heard of witchcraft and the Evil Eye".

Hawker's works are full of references to charms, spells, occult lore and practices, as this last tale demonstrates. This does beg the question: where did all this information come from? One could speculate that it came from people such as Old Cherry herself but I hear you protest that without empirical evidence such speculation is meaningless. Well maybe the 'smoking gun' is an old label found in the archives and that once accompanied a picture of Hawker in the Museum of Witchcraft and Magic. It also, interestingly, refers to an occult practice dearly-held by Cecil Williamson, the founder of the museum, and in a variant form also became a mainstay of the pagan religion of Wicca.

"Two pictures of the Reverend S Hawker, one in full church vestment and the other at the front door of his church in Morwenstow, North Cornwall, not far from Hartland Point. This extraordinarily colourful priest was doubly interested in the spirit world of afterlife and to that end he made a point of winning the friendship of witches in his locality. One such was old Cherry who lived nearby. She it was who introduced him to the witch's art of calling down the moon."

Tamsin Blight

No account of West Country cunning folk would be complete without a reference to Cornwall's most famous witch – Tamsin/Thomasine Blight – known in her own life time as Tammy Blee, 'The White Witch of Helston' and 'The Witch of the West'.

Unlike many of her sisters in the arte, her life is relatively well-documented. We have accounts of her life from the 19th-century folklorists William Bottrell and Robert Hunt, and in the 20th century from William Paynter, Kelvin Jones and Jason Semmens.

She was born in 1798 at Gwennap, in the heartlands of Cornwall's tin mining industry. It is not known when her practice of the magical artes began, but in 1835 she was living in the mining town of Redruth and married the cunning man James or Jemmy Thomas of Illogan. He had a dubious reputation and was the subject of a number of tabloid-esque newspaper articles regarding what many considered to be his fraudulent practices, not least that of asking his male clients to sleep with him as part of their 'cure'! It was as a result of an incident in which he tried to persuade a burly St Ives fisherman called Mr Paynter "to commit a disgraceful offence" that eventually led to his separation from Tamsin Blight.

She subsequently made the intriguing statement that: "The Virtue was in her not in him; that she was of real peller blood, and that he could tell nothing but through her". This is significant for a number of reasons. Firstly, because while with Thomas she had already begun to practice as a cunning woman and had established a good reputation; it was at this point she really becomes an independent practitioner. Secondly, she uses the terms 'virtue' and 'peller'. This is the first time we see the term peller popularly used as an epithet for white witch. In another tale, told by both Hunt and Bottrell, the lineage of pellers came from a man called Lutey from The Lizard, who in turn won his gift from a mermaid. She also introduces the concept of 'virtue'; in this context it does not refer to ethics or morality, but draws upon its archaic meaning as a kind of 'energy' that defines something as a magical entity – call it 'prana' or 'the breath of the dragon' or what you will – it is the stuff that makes a peller!

In the mid-19th century she set up a high-street practice in the well-to-do Cornish market town of Helston. The grand granite-built terraced building can still be seen a couple of doors down the hill from the 'Blue Anchor' inn. People would come from far and wide to visit her, including tinners and seamen before they commenced on a new seam or voyage. In 1870 William Bottrell gives a vivid description of the scene as the crowds came in the spring to 'recharge' their charms given by the peller in the previous year. Oddly, he refers to Tammy Blee as a man: "Though they arrived at the Pellar's at the forenoon, such a crowd was already assembled that they waited long before their turn came to be admitted in to the presence of the Wiseman. The conjurer received the people and their offerings, singly, in to the room by courtesy styled the hale (hall). Few remained closeted for more than half-an-hour, during which time they were provided with little bags of earth, teeth or bones taken from the grave. These precious relics were to be worn suspended from the neck, for the prevention of fits and other mysterious complaints brought on by witchcraft".

Bottrell goes on to describe a number of her charms and spells, and also some tales relating to her exploits as a jobbing peller. Not only was she a purveyor of charms and spells, she also had the ability to both heal and curse. She was a respected fortune-teller and as an exorcist had the ability to both raise spirits and lay them to rest. In one tale in which she is called upon to recover a missing legacy she replies: "But you know this is a dreadful thing to undertake, and I shall want some money – two pounds at least – that we may get herbs, drugs and other things not easily procured". This one sentence gives us an insight not only into her working methods but also the kind of money she was making. Two pounds would have been roughly a month's wages to a labourer at that time.

In 1856 she passed away and was buried in the Helston parish churchyard. It was said that after her funeral a great storm swept across Helston and the afternoon was as black as night. Some folks said it was the 'Old One' saluting her as she passed over. It could be said that Tammy Blee set the bar for all West Country pellers to come. In 1895, in an auction in Penzance, an oil painting (possibly by one of the Opies) of Tammy Blee turned up. She is depicted as a mature lady wearing a bonnet and floral shawl, and she has a somewhat pensive expression on her face and enigmatically cradles a small silver box in her hands. It is now owned by the Royal Cornwall Museum in Truro, and when on display she stands with the great and the good of Cornwall looking out over the people as they come and go, like an elder statesperson of the cunning tradition.

APPENDIX A

The Old Charms from the 'Wise Woman's Cottage': 1998-2015

This collection of spoken charms and spells was collected and compiled by Levannah Morgan (author and founder of the 'Friends of the Museum of Witchcraft') and were voiced by Cassandra Latham (author and "Witch of Buryan"). They were played in the 'Wise Woman's Cottage' for a period stretching between 1998 and 2015.

The explanatory notes are taken directly from a CD which was produced on an occasional basis by Graham King for the Museum of Witchcraft and Magic. For those without notes, the spell is usually quite self-explanatory. The charms themselves are an eclectic and evocative collection drawn from the charms used by a witches' coven in mid-Devon in the 1990s. These in turn were drawn from the folklore of

Britain and America, their own arcane traditions and more recent Wiccan sources and woven together in a potent witch's skein!

1. The Witch's Ladder: this spell is recited while tying nine knots in a string or rope. Feathers, cloth or hair are sometimes tied into the knots.

"By knot of one the spell's begun.
By knot of two, the spell is true.
By knot of three, so mote it be.
By knot of four, the open door.
By knot of five, the spell's alive.
By knot of six, the spell I fix.
By knot of seven, the gates of heaven.
By knot of eight, the hand of fate.
By knot of nine, the spell be mine!"

2. A spell used by Cornish pellers to cure burns:

"There were three ladies came out of the West.
Two for fire, one for frost.
Out with thee fire, in with thee frost!"
3. A spell used to shapeshift in to a hare.

First recorded in the Confessions of Isobel Gowdie (1662):

"I shall go in to a hare,
With sorrow and sighing and mickle care;
And I shall go in the Horned God's name,
Aye, 'til I come home again."

4. Many spells used the four elements; this old spell needs no explanation:

"Power of wind I have over thee.
Power of flame I have over thee.
Power of wave I have over thee.
Power of earth I have over thee!"

5. Used while visualising the person on whom the spell is to be cast:

"I speak to you and bid you hear.
I speak to you and bid you here."

6. Wishing on a star – simple ancient magic:

"Star light, star bright,
First star that I see tonight.

I wish I may, I wish I might,
Have the wish I wish tonight."

7. Wind could be raised by whipping a cord or rag against a rock. A similar spell is recorded in the Confessions of Isobel Gowdie (1662):

"I knock this rag upon this stone,
To raise this storm in the Horned One's name.
It shall not lie till I please again."

8. " … And if they came not on the first night, then do the same on the second night until they do come, for doubtless they will come. And lay thou in thy bed, and look thou have a fair silken handkerchief about thy head, and be not afraid for they will do thee no harm. For there will come before thee three fair women, and all in white clothing, and one shall put a ring upon your finger, wherewith thou shall go invisible. When thou hast the ring upon thy finger, look in a glass, and thou shall not see thyself."

9. "Now with magic howlings she keeps the swarms of the grave before her; now she sprinkles them with milk and bids them retreat."

10. A classic protection charm:

"Black-luggie, Hammer-head
Rowan tree and red thread,
Put the warlocks to their speed."

11. A spell used to shapeshift in to a crow, from the Confessions of Isobel Gowdie (1662):

"I shall go into a crow,
With sorrow and such and black throe;
I shall go in the Horned Lord's name,
Aye 'til I come home again."

12. "Take the gall of a cat and hen's fat,
Mixing them together,
Put this on your eyes and you will
See things that are invisible to others."

13. A version of the well-known incantation to be said while seeing a

magpie. Magpies have always been considered magical birds:

"One for sorrow
Two for mirth
Three for a wedding
And four for a birth
Five for silver
Six for gold
And seven for a secret that has never been told."

14. The village wise woman would always provide good, practical help for the community, for casting the weather was an important service to the rural population:

"If Candlemas be fair and bright,
Winter will have another flight;
But if Candlemas day be clouds and rain,
Winter is gone and will not come again."

15. "Pale moon do rain, red moon do blow. White moon do neither rain nor snow."

16. This confirms how lucky it is to find a four-leaf clover!

"One for fame and one for wealth
And one for a faithful lover,
And one to bring you glorious health
And all are in a four-leaf clover."

17. To bless a house, a protection charm:

"This bag I sow with luck for me,
And also for my family,
That it may keep by night and day
Trouble and illness far away.
Flag, Flax, Fodder and Frig."

18. "Speak no evil, write no ill,
May the heart and hands be still.
As I bind – this is my will."

19. "Upon this candle I will write,
What I wish of thee this night.
As the runes of magic flow,
With the mind and flame aglow,
I trust that thou will grant this boon,
Gracious Goddess of the moon."

20. An extremely old healing spell. A German (sic) version of this spell was found in the 9th century.

"This is the spell that I intone,
Flesh to flesh and bone to bone,
Sinew to sinew and vein to vein,
And each one will be whole again."

21. "I call to earth to bind my spell,
Air speed its travel well.
Fire gives it spirit from above,
Water quenches this spell with love."

22. "Fire flame and fire burn,
Make the mill of magic turn.
Work the will for which I pray,
Io Dio Ha Hey Hey!

Air breath and air blow,
Make the mill of magic go.
Work the will for which we pray,
Io Dio Ha Hey Hey!

Water heat and water boil,
Make the mill of magic toil.

Work the will for which I pray,
Io Dio Ha Hey Hey!

Earth without and earth within,
Make the mill of magic spin.
Work the will for which I pray,
Io Dio Ha Hey Hey!

23. "Ashen tree, ashen tree
I pray you buy this wart from me."

24. To conclude or seal a spell. It can be
recited while tying a knot.
"I wind, I bind,
This spell be mine."

25. "Candle shining in the night
With your flame enchanted,
By the powers of magic might
May this wish be granted.
When the candle sheds its gleam
At the mystic hour,
Let fulfilment of my dream
Gather mystic power.
Flame of magic brightly burn,
Spirit of the fire,
Let the wheel of fortune turn,

Grant me my desire.
One, two, three – so shall it be!"

26. "Yarrow, sweet yarrow,
The first I have found.
In the name of Hornie
I pluck you from the ground.
By wind and flame and wave and tree,
Grant the thing I wish to me."

27. "By Robbin son of arte
And our good lady of the moon,
By the sun that shines for us,
Grant me my will.
So mote it be."

28. "As merry we have met,
And merry have we been,
So merry may we part,
And merry meet again."

APPENDIX B

Wayside Witches of the Museum of Witchcraft & Magic

Cecil Williamson explained: "For years I have been doing fieldwork, seeking out 'grass-roots' workers of magic, wise women and witches, call them what you will". He claimed to have been in contact with 82 Aunty Mays in his researches but the only details that remain of them are those which are woven in to the fabric of his museum. Most of the informants remain anonymous, forgotten and unverifiable, but this is understandable due to the nature of the material. Even in this modern age there is still a great deal of suspicion of witchcraft, and the persecutions still go on! One such informant who was 'outed', the dance teacher Brownie Pate (who now has a display dedicated to her in the Museum of Witchcraft and Magic) was hounded from her job and lambasted by the press as a result of her involvement with witchcraft being made public. To this day, for family and work reasons, many donors of artefacts and informants to the Museum of Witchcraft and Magic wish to remain anonymous. However, it seems that Cecil Williamson was often inclined to encode the actual names and places relating to the artefacts in to the accompanying script. Maybe this was another aspect of his working technique that harked back to his time spent in MI6!

That said, among the old display labels of the museum there are a number of cunning folk, Aunty Mays and other assorted practitioners of the arte who have actually been named. There is no further information about them than that on the label; in most cases this consists of little more than a name, an associated artefact, an approximate location (most of them seem to be from Devon and Cornwall) and the date of collection of the item. In some cases the artefacts are still on display and you may be able to find them around the museum; in other cases the associated artefact has long gone and only the label remains in the museum archive. Perhaps in time their tales will reveal themselves to us, but in the meantime, in no particular order, here is the list.

• Liza Pengelly of Saltash – 'get-lost' box in a stocking
• Sarah Noaks of Crewkerne – 'Ben' the dried frog familiar (1922)
• Dora of St Ives – 'Fred' the familiar in a beaded box
• Dorothea May 'Dodo' of Plymouth – lucky coins
• 'Eggy Baldhead' Roberts, the stonemason, warlock and cunning man – skull and dagger
• Betty Downes of Budleigh Salterton – Wooden wishbox (1928)
• Old Hannah of Moretonhampstead – flint elf-shot for divination
• Nancy of Newlyn – divination by belemnites or 'devils thunderbolts'
• Kate 'the Gull' Turner of Penryn – divinatory tambourine

- Kathy Collins of Kit Hill near Callington, Cornwall – divinatory quartz balls
- Betty Coles of Umberleigh – egg-tipped wand (late 1920s)
- Old Granny Mann of North Bovey – skull mounted on star-shaped stand
- Smelly Nelly of Paignton – black moon crystal ball
- Young Sarah of Mary Tavy – wax poppet-making equipment (1963)
- Joan Wytte, the 'Fighting Fairy Woman of Bodmin' – skeleton (1775)
- Charity West/Old Cherry of Welcombe – mortar and pestle
- Joan Long, a traveller in the West Country – the healing 'Fanny stone'
- Singing Sal – healing lead heart
- Dora Evans of Dinan Mawddy – ill-wishing shrine collected from 'peller man'
- Jane Langden of Nanpean – famous 'get-lost' boxes
- Sylvia Stone of Chard – healing wooden breast on chain (1946)
- Mrs Sally Semmens, the 'Green Witch' of Wells – healing leaden breast

- Pansy Parsons of Helston – small cauldron
- Rhoda Roberts of Exeter – painted 17th-century talisman (1910)
- Sandy Brown of Torrington – Tosh the stoat! (1932)
- Mrs Delaney-Brown, the witch and necromancer of Maida Vale – Tibetan collection
- Amelia Reardon, the 'Well-to-do Witch' of Edgware Road (London) – black velvet bag and dark crystal (1898)
- Marie, the witch of Marseilles
- Martha Hyde of Newington – silver charm (Lovett Collection)
- Joan Morgan, the herbalist of Swanscombe in Kent – elder
- Black Doris, the charmer of Union Street, Plymouth – she-sparrow jealousy charm
- Audrey Rundle of Norton Fitzwarren near Taunton – leather cattle stroker
- Jane Rowe/Rouse of Newlyn – mercury weather-charming bottle
- Mrs Bell, 'Fairy Bell' of Mary Tavy (died 1926) – familiar
- Mother Leakey, the sea-witch of

Porlock – knotted rope charm
• Bessy Bensons of Ottery St Mary –
flint dagger
• Sarah Killier of Santon on the Isle
of Man – cauldron, pot and chain
(recovered 1954)
• Widow Morley, the charmer of
Atcham near Shrewsbury – mole's foot
charm
• Mary Nutter, the last of the Lancashire
witches – replica of witch's cottage
(1856- 1928)
• Mrs Bone, the witch of Tooting,
London – Eastern collection
• Madam De Lyon of Paris – spirit-
house
• Peter Howard of Hadley in Essex –
'get-lost' box
• Tommy 'Old Nick' Nicholls of
Sissinghurst – native seed necklace
• Richard Adams, the charmer of
Manningtree, Essex – black penny
charm (1930)
• Ben Tucker of Crowborough, Sussex –
black penny charm (1936)
• Charley Wallace of Rockcliffe near Carlisle
– silver coins in sunrise-water charm

- Jim Clowes of Campten near Evesham – ferret's head anti-theft charm (1929)
- Old Jim Crow of the Isle of Man – black holed-charm
- Fred Larkin, the 'Green Doctor' of Norwich – glass, candle and penny charm, and pin and candle charm
- Old Katie of Honiton – lace-makers' glass spirit-house
- Molly 'the Golly' of Highgate, London – charms on collared silks
- Bessy Brooks, the West Country travelling charmer – leather divination mat (1930s)
- Willey Cox of Great Shefford – holed coins (1881)
- John Longmore, the charmer of Jedbourough – black coins
- John Green, the herbal charmer of Alderminster near Stratford-on-Avon (1920s)
- Geo Dennis, the charmer of Evesham – bracelet of zinc, copper and brass (1934)
- George Latimer of Bishopstone, Sussex – vagina flint charm
- 'Old Tom Dobbie', the Sussex horse

doctor – velvet bag with iron pyrites
• Tom Allard of Shepton Mallet –
ointment (1930s)
• Mrs Alice Tonkin, 'Killer Tonkin' the
witch of Redruth – cat familiar (1910)
• Letty Toms, the West Country
travelling fortune-teller (old but alive in
1960s) – pack of cards 'cat'

Further Reading

Three great little booklets (if you can get hold
of them) on Cornish cunning folk:

Jones, Kelvin. *Seven Cornish Witches*, 1998

Mullins, Rose. *White Witches – a Study of Charmers*

Semmens, Jason. *The Witch of the West*, 2004

A good collection of traditional charms can be
found in:

Hewett, Sarah. *Nummits & Crummits: Devonshire Customs, Characteristics, and Folk-Lore,* 1900

King, Graham. *The British Book of Spells & Charms – A Compilation of Traditional Folk Magic,* (Troy Books) 2016

Paynter, William. Ed Semmens, Jason *The Cornish Witch-finder,* (The Federation of Old Cornwall Societies) 2008

For an in-depth historical account of the wayside witch:

Davies, Owen. *Popular Magic – Cunning Folk in English History*, (Hambledon Continuum) 2007

Froome, Joyce. *Wicked Enchantments – A History of the Pendle Witches & their Magic*, (Palatine Books) 2010

Howard, Michael. *West Country Witches,* (Three Hands Press) 2010. Part of a series covering Wales, Scotland and East Anglia.

Thomas, Kieth. *Religion & the Decline of Magic,* (Penguin University Books) 1973

For accounts of contemporary cunning magical practice:

Gary, Gemma. *Traditional Witchcraft – A Cornish Book of Ways,* (Troy Books) 2008

– *The Black Toad* (Troy Books) 2012

Morgan, Levannah. *A Witch's Mirror – the Art of Making Magic,* (Capall Bann) 2013

For accounts of modern cunning practitioners:

Howard, Michael. *Children of Cain – A Study of Modern Traditional Witchcraft* (Three Hands Press) 2011

Various authors. *Serpent Songs,* (Scarlet Imprint) 2013

For an in-depth account of Cecil Williamson, the Museum of Witchcraft, and the cunning practices of the wayside witch:

Hannat, Sarah. Costin, Simon. *Of Shadows – One Hundred Objects from the Museum of Witchcraft & Magic,* (Strange Attractor Press) 2016

Patterson, Steve. *Cecil Williamson's Book of Witchcraft – A Grimoire of the Museum of Witchcraft,* (Troy Books) 2014

For a quick 'geek' into the world of Cornish folklore:

Courtney, M. A. *Cornish Feasts & Folklore,* 1890

Dean, Tony. Shaw, Tony. *Folklore of Cornwall,* (Tempus) 2003

For the folklore of England, including much magical lore:

Westwood, J. Simpson, J. *The Lore of the Land –* J Westwood and J Simpson (Penguin) 2006